GLOBAL
KNIFE CULTURE

HUMANITY'S MOST VERSATILE CREATION

TOM SOTIS

Global Knife Culture

ISBN # 978-1-300-88387-6

Imprint: Lulu.com

To my good friend

Mattias Persson

Contents

Introduction

From ancient civilizations to modern urban landscapes, knives have played a vital role in shaping human societies. They are among humanity's earliest tools, used for hunting, food preparation, and defense. Yet knives also hold profound cultural, symbolic, and martial significance, and across the globe, the ways in which societies have developed and ritualized knife usage reveal much about human adaptation, cultural values, and survival instincts. *Global Knife Culture* seeks to explore the multifaceted roles of knives across continents, tracing their journey from utilitarian objects to revered weapons of art and honor.

The significance of the knife extends far beyond its function. In some cultures, knives have spiritual meanings, representing power, protection, and warrior spirit. For example, the karambit of Southeast Asia is not just a curved, claw-like blade but also a symbol of the tiger's ferocity and prowess. Its origins are deeply intertwined with agricultural life, but it has become an emblem of stealth and precision in martial traditions. Similarly, the Kukri of Nepal, wielded by the legendary Gurkha warriors, stands as a testament to a culture that values bravery and tenacity, with ceremonies and myths reinforcing its almost sacred status.

Knife combat traditions are equally diverse and fascinating. In the Philippines, the blade arts of Kali and Eskrima teach not only the practicalities of knife fighting but also principles of movement, awareness, and respect for the blade. Here, knives are seen as extensions of the body, and combat drills are passed down from generation to generation, preserving the rich heritage of a warrior culture. In contrast, Japanese tantojutsu reflects the ritualistic and codified nature of samurai martial practices, emphasizing precise strikes and discipline. The cultural philosophies embedded in these traditions—whether the Filipino emphasis on adaptability or the Japanese reverence for form—reveal much about how societies interpret the nature of combat and self-defense.

Even in Western contexts, knives carry layered meanings. In places like Scotland, the sgian-dubh—a small, single-edged knife worn with traditional Highland dress—has roots that evoke both functionality and status. The practice of wearing the sgian-dubh is linked to a complex history of hospitality and readiness, illustrating the intertwined relationship between social customs and knife culture. Meanwhile, in Italy, the stiletto knife emerged as a product of Renaissance craftsmanship, a time when personal defense and political intrigue went hand in hand. The stiletto's slender and elegant design became synonymous with the art of dueling and honor, marking a chapter where knives were instruments of personal and family pride.

Yet knife culture is not confined to the past. In today's globalized world, knives remain an integral part of our identity, evolving in design and purpose. In some areas, knives are status symbols, treasured heirlooms passed down with family histories, while in other regions, they are utilitarian tools essential for daily life, whether for food preparation, crafts, or wilderness survival. The modern tactical knife movement, with its focus on innovation and self-defense, reflects contemporary anxieties and a renewed interest in personal empowerment and safety. Brands and makers have cultivated passionate followings, demonstrating that knives are still objects of fascination and cultural pride.

The controversial aspect of knives cannot be overlooked. The criminalization of knife ownership in some urban centers and the rise of knife-related violence in others have sparked debates on security, legislation, and the ethics of self-defense. Across the world, laws and regulations differ widely, often influenced by historical and social factors. For instance, strict laws in the United Kingdom, aimed at curbing knife crime, highlight societal struggles with violence and protection, while knife-carrying customs in rural areas of countries like Finland continue to be part of everyday life.

Global Knife Culture is also about the artisans and innovators who craft these weapons and tools. Knife-making traditions, such as the celebrated Damascus steel of the Middle East or the contemporary artistry of custom blade smiths, underscore a deep appreciation for materials and craftsmanship. The process of forging a blade—transforming raw metal into something functional and beautiful—embodies the human spirit of creativity and ingenuity. Cultural stories and the dedicated individuals behind them, from master blacksmiths in Japan to makers innovating with synthetic materials, illustrate a dynamic interplay between heritage and innovation.

This book will journey through the knife cultures of the world, offering insights into how knives influence daily lives, ceremonial practices, self-defense systems, and national identities. It will delve into the philosophies and customs that surround these weapons, highlighting both the beauty and the brutality embedded in the blade. In doing so, *Global Knife Culture* provides an immersive look into the power and paradox of one of humanity's most enduring creations.

Prepare to embark on a journey that cuts through time, geography, and tradition, unraveling the narratives, artistry, and human values embedded in the blade. Whether you are a martial artist, a historian, a craftsman, or simply someone intrigued by human culture, this book invites you to explore the deep and often surprising world of knives.

North America

Knife culture in North American countries—primarily the United States, Canada, and Mexico—is diverse and influenced by historical, cultural, and practical needs, spanning from indigenous traditions to modern self-defense and tactical applications. Knives serve as essential tools, symbols of identity, and weapons, reflecting both rural and urban lifestyles. Here's an overview of knife culture in North America:

United States

Historical Roots and Frontier Culture: Knife culture in the U.S. has strong roots in the frontier and pioneering era, where knives like the Bowie knife gained popularity. These large, versatile blades were used by pioneers, frontiersmen, and soldiers, embodying the rugged, self-sufficient spirit of early American life.

The Bowie Knife: Named after Jim Bowie, the Bowie knife has become iconic in American culture, symbolizing strength, resilience, and independence. Its reputation is closely tied to duels and skirmishes of the 19th century, and it has since influenced modern knife designs in both form and function.

Modern Tactical Knife Culture: The U.S. has a strong tactical knife culture, popular among military, law enforcement, and civilian self-defense enthusiasts. Companies like Benchmade, Spyderco, and Ka-Bar have developed tactical folding knives and fixed blades used worldwide for personal protection, survival, and utility.

Everyday Carry (EDC) Movement: Knives are integral to the EDC community in the U.S., with many Americans carrying compact folding knives daily. EDC culture values preparedness and practicality, with knives used for everything from opening packages to emergency situations. Popular EDC knives include models from brands like Leatherman, Gerber, and Victorinox.

Martial Arts Influence: Knife-based martial arts such as Filipino Kali and Escrima have become popular in the U.S., with systems that focus on edged-weapon defense and offense. Additionally, American instructors have developed systems like Martial Blade Concepts (MBC), blending principles from multiple knife-fighting traditions with a focus on practical self-defense.

Canada

Utility and Wilderness Survival: Canada's vast wilderness makes knives essential for outdoor survival, camping, and hunting. Canadians commonly carry robust fixed-blade knives and folding knives for tasks related to hunting, fishing, and preparing food in remote areas. Brands like Grohmann (known for its Canadian Belt Knife) are popular for their durability and versatility in rugged conditions.

Indigenous Knife Traditions: Canada's indigenous communities have long-standing knife traditions, including the use of the *ulu*, a crescent-shaped knife used by Inuit communities for skinning and preparing food. Knives in indigenous cultures often hold ceremonial value and are made with materials reflecting the local environment, such as bone and stone.

Regulation and EDC: Canadian knife laws are stricter than those in the U.S., with prohibitions on automatic knives and knives intended for self-defense. Many Canadians carry folding knives as part of EDC, focusing on tools that are practical rather than overtly tactical due to legal restrictions.

Martial Arts and Self-Defense: Knife-based martial arts, especially those rooted in Filipino and Western styles, have gained popularity, with practitioners interested in self-defense training and edged-weapon defense. Schools across Canada teach techniques for knife defense, and organizations offer training on how to handle knives safely in survival or combative contexts.

Mexico

Historical and Cultural Significance: In Mexico, knives have both practical and symbolic significance. The *machete* is an essential tool in agricultural regions, used for clearing vegetation and performing other tasks. It's also a symbol of rural life, often associated with farmers, indigenous communities, and revolutionaries.

The Machete as a Weapon and Tool: Due to its prevalence and accessibility, the machete is widely used for self-defense in rural areas. It has also been a symbol of resistance, historically wielded by peasants during revolutionary movements. For many, it represents the resilience and determination of rural Mexicans.

Everyday Carry and Street Culture: In urban Mexico, smaller folding knives are common as everyday carry items, used for practical purposes or personal safety. In areas with high crime rates, knives are sometimes seen as tools of self-defense. Street vendors and craftsmen often carry compact knives for daily tasks.

Lucha con Cuchillo (Knife Fighting): Mexican street fighting sometimes includes *lucha con cuchillo*, an informal style of knife fighting that focuses on quick, practical techniques. Though not a formalized martial art, this style is influenced by necessity and urban life, often blending indigenous knife skills with street survival tactics.

Interest in Filipino Martial Arts (FMA): Like in the U.S., Filipino martial arts have grown in popularity in Mexico. Practitioners study Kali and Escrima as methods for knife combat and self-defense, focusing on blade work and defensive techniques that can be adapted to real-life situations.

Common Themes Across North America

Preparedness and Survival: In all three countries, knives are essential for survival, particularly in rural and wilderness areas. From Canadian hunters to American outdoorsmen and Mexican farmers, knives serve as indispensable tools for those who live and work in natural settings.

Cultural Identity and Symbolism: Knives are often symbolic, representing independence, resilience, and cultural heritage. The Bowie knife in the U.S., the machete in Mexico, and the ulu among Canada's indigenous people all reflect cultural pride and self-reliance.

Self-Defense and Practical EDC: Knife culture across North America includes a practical focus on self-defense. In the U.S., knives are commonly carried for personal protection, while in Canada and Mexico, where laws are stricter, knives tend to be carried more for utility than for tactical purposes.

Martial Arts and Tactical Training: Filipino Martial Arts (FMA) have become highly influential across North America. Systems like Kali and Escrima have gained widespread recognition, with schools offering knife-based self-defense courses. Additionally, American instructors have developed their own combative systems, such as AMOK! and MBC, often combining principles from FMA with tactical adaptations.

Regulation and Legal Influence

Knife regulations vary significantly across North America. In the United States, knife laws are more lenient in some states, allowing tactical knives and a variety of EDC blades, while certain states have restrictions. Canada has stricter laws, with many tactical knives prohibited, and Mexican laws vary but generally restrict carrying weapons in public.

Despite these regulations, knife culture remains robust, with many enthusiasts finding ways to legally incorporate knives into their daily lives, focusing on utility and preparedness while adhering to legal guidelines.

Modern Knife Culture and Technology

Customization and Knife Collecting: Across North America, knife customization and collecting have become popular. High-quality, custom-made knives are highly sought after, with many North Americans willing to invest in unique designs from well-known makers. Brands like Benchmade, Spyderco, Buck, and Cold Steel have large followings.

EDC and Tactical Gear: The rise of the EDC community in the U.S. and Canada has popularized carrying knives as part of everyday preparedness. EDC knives are designed to be compact, durable, and multifunctional, appealing to individuals who value preparedness and functionality.

Online Communities and Education: Knife culture in North America has a strong online presence, with forums, social media groups, and YouTube channels dedicated to knife reviews, techniques, and EDC tips. This online culture has fostered a sense of community, where enthusiasts exchange knowledge and promote responsible knife use.

Summary

Knife culture in North America blends historical tradition, practical utility, and modern tactical innovations. From the heritage of the Bowie knife to the cultural pride in the machete and the functional, minimalist EDC movement, knives continue to hold a place of importance across the continent. Whether as tools of survival, symbols of identity, or instruments of self-defense, knives remain an integral part of North American culture.

Central America

Knife culture in Central American countries is similarly rich and multifaceted, reflecting indigenous traditions, colonial influences, agricultural practices, and the need for personal defense. Knives play a prominent role as tools, symbols, and defensive weapons in both rural and urban environments across the region. Here's an overview of knife culture across several Central American countries:

Guatemala

The Machete as an All-Purpose Tool: In Guatemala, the machete is an essential tool for agricultural work, used by farmers and rural laborers for clearing land, harvesting crops, and other tasks. In rural Mayan communities, the machete is often a part of daily life and cultural identity.

Symbol of Rural Life and Defense: Beyond its role as a tool, the machete is also a symbol of resilience and defense. Many rural Guatemalans carry it for personal protection, particularly in regions where law enforcement is scarce.

Knife and Machete Fighting Arts: Some indigenous and local practices have developed around machete fighting techniques, influenced by necessity and self-defense. These techniques are often taught informally and emphasize simple, effective movements meant to protect and counter an aggressor quickly.

El Salvador

Street and Gang Influence: Knives, including switchblades, folding knives, and machetes, are commonly used by street gangs and have become a part of urban violence in El Salvador. The prevalence of gang violence has led to knives being associated with personal defense in high-risk areas.

Everyday Carry: Many Salvadorans, particularly in rural regions, carry knives for everyday tasks and self-defense. A folding knife or small blade is a practical tool in both urban and rural life, given the often limited access to law enforcement.

Machete Symbolism: In the countryside, the machete is not only a tool but also a symbol of rural life and resistance. It represents strength, resilience, and the spirit of rural Salvadoran culture, often associated with campesinos (farmers) and their way of life.

Honduras

Machete as a Common Tool and Weapon: As in other Central American countries, the machete in Honduras is a vital tool for agricultural work. Farmers and laborers rely on it for clearing vegetation, harvesting, and various other tasks. It is also a common weapon for self-defense in both rural and urban settings.

Martial Influence and Training: Although not widespread, some Honduran martial arts and self-defense schools have begun to incorporate knife and machete defense techniques. This is often in response to high crime rates and the prevalence of knife-related violence, especially in urban areas.

Cultural Significance: The machete symbolizes the strength and resilience of Honduran people, particularly those living in rural areas. Many see it as a symbol of their connection to the land and their ability to defend themselves if necessary.

Nicaragua

Machetes in Daily Life and Conflict: In Nicaragua, the machete is an everyday tool, especially in the rural areas where it's used for farming, clearing fields, and other work. It has also been used in local conflicts and confrontations, especially in isolated areas with limited police presence.

Street Knife Defense: In urban areas, knives are frequently used in street altercations, both by civilians for self-defense and by gangs or criminals. Knife culture in cities has led to a growing interest in self-defense techniques, with some schools and instructors focusing on practical knife defenses.

Ritual and Indigenous Significance: In some indigenous Nicaraguan communities, knives hold ceremonial significance and are often passed down through generations. These knives are typically smaller and more decorative than the utilitarian machetes used in daily life.

Costa Rica

The Peasant Knife (Peón Knife): In Costa Rican agricultural communities, smaller utility knives known as *peón* knives are commonly used for farming, harvesting, and everyday tasks. These knives are a practical and cultural staple, associated with the hardworking peasant life.

Machete in the Countryside: The machete is a mainstay in Costa Rican farming and rural communities, used as a versatile tool and, if needed, a defensive weapon. In regions with a strong connection to the land, the machete holds a symbolic role, representing both livelihood and self-sufficiency.

Growing Interest in Self-Defense: While Costa Rica has lower violent crime rates than some of its neighbors, there is increasing interest in self-defense, including knife defense techniques. Many Costa Ricans view self-defense training as a practical response to the risks that come with urbanization and tourism.

Panama

Knife Culture in Indigenous Communities: Panama is home to several indigenous groups, such as the Guna and Emberá, who incorporate knives and small blades into their daily lives and cultural practices. Knives are often used for crafting, hunting, and ceremonial purposes.

Machete for Agriculture and Defense: The machete is widely used in rural Panamanian areas for agricultural work and also as a weapon for self-defense. Many rural Panamanians are skilled in handling machetes, and they see it as both a tool and a means of protection.

Urban Knife Use: In cities, knives are often carried for personal safety. The need for self-defense is particularly strong in areas with higher crime rates, leading to a streetwise culture of knife handling among some Panamanian civilians.

Belize

Multicultural Knife Traditions: Belize's knife culture is shaped by its diverse population, including Creole, Maya, and Garifuna influences. Each group has unique uses and practices involving knives, often tied to hunting, fishing, and agriculture.

Machete as a Tool and Cultural Symbol: In Belizean rural communities, the machete is essential for farming and land clearing. For many, it represents self-reliance and resourcefulness, particularly in rural areas where it's central to daily life.

Self-Defense and Survival: With a growing interest in survival skills and self-defense, many Belizeans see the machete and smaller knives as essential survival tools. These knives are carried not just for utility but also as a form of protection, particularly in remote areas.

Common Themes Across Central America

Agricultural Significance: The machete is the most prominent knife in Central American culture, especially in rural areas where farming is a way of life. It's not only a tool but also a symbol of rural identity, hard work, and resilience across these countries.

Knives for Personal Defense: In both urban and rural settings, knives are often the weapon of choice for personal defense. High crime rates in some areas mean that many people, especially in cities, carry small knives or folding blades as a precaution.

Indigenous and Ceremonial Uses: Many indigenous groups in Central America have traditions involving knives, where they are used in ceremonies, hunting, and crafting. These practices add a cultural dimension to knife use beyond their practical functions.

Influence of Crime and Gang Activity: In urban areas of countries like El Salvador, Honduras, and Guatemala, knives are commonly associated with gang violence, leading to both practical and defensive knife use among civilians.

Summary

The knife culture in Central America is deeply interwoven with practical needs, cultural identity, and the realities of safety and survival. While the machete is a unifying symbol across the region, smaller knives also play essential roles in both daily life and self-defense, highlighting the knife's versatility and importance in Central American societies.

South America

Knife culture in South American countries has deep historical and cultural roots, with knives often serving as tools, symbols of identity, and weapons of self-defense. Each country has unique knife traditions influenced by indigenous practices, European colonization, and local innovations. Here's a look at knife culture across several South American countries:

Argentina

The Gaucho and the Facón: Argentina's gaucho (cowboy) culture is central to its knife traditions. The *facón*—a large, single-edged knife with a long blade—is an iconic tool and weapon for gauchos, used for daily tasks, food preparation, and as a defensive weapon.

Dueling Traditions: Knife duels, or *duelos criollos*, were historically a part of gaucho culture, with elaborate dueling rituals where the facón was wielded both as a weapon and a symbol of honor. These duels were typically fought to first blood, but in some cases could be fatal.

Martial Arts Influence: Today, there are Argentine martial arts such as *esgrima criolla* that preserve facón fighting techniques. Practitioners study historical techniques and principles of gaucho knife fighting, often as a way to keep traditional skills alive.

Brazil

Capoeira and the Navalha: The *navalha*, or straight razor, became a popular self-defense weapon among practitioners of *Capoeira* in urban Brazil. The navalha was favored due to its concealability and ease of access, especially in urban environments.

Cangaceiros and Knives: In Brazil's northeastern region, *cangaceiros* (bandits) in the early 20th century carried large knives, often called *peixeira*, as tools and weapons. These knives were essential for their rugged lifestyle in the *sertão* (backcountry), and they became symbols of rebellion and resistance against authority.

Modern Martial Arts: Brazilian knife fighting, while less formalized than in some cultures, has been incorporated into modern martial arts, especially within self-defense systems that mix Brazilian Jiu-Jitsu and other disciplines with practical knife techniques for personal safety.

Chile

The Corvo: The *corvo* is a distinctive, curved knife traditionally associated with Chilean soldiers and still used in ceremonial contexts today. Historically used by Chilean troops, particularly during the War of the Pacific, the corvo is known for its inward curve, resembling a talon or hook.

Military Influence: The corvo is often a symbol of patriotism and national pride, and some Chilean military units still train in its use. It has become a part of Chile's cultural identity, with modern adaptations available for collectors and enthusiasts.

Popular Self-Defense: In rural and urban areas alike, knives are commonly used as tools, but they also serve as self-defense weapons. Many Chileans learn basic knife handling as a means of personal protection, especially in high-crime areas.

Colombia

The Machete as a Tool and Weapon: In Colombia, the machete is a vital tool for farmers and laborers, especially in rural areas, where it is used for agriculture, clearing brush, and other tasks. However, it also serves as a weapon for self-defense and is sometimes associated with territorial disputes in rural areas.

Influence on Street Fighting: In urban areas, knives are often the weapon of choice for street self-defense. *Pico e pala* (meaning "beak and shovel") is a local term referring to Colombian street knife-fighting techniques that prioritize quick, defensive movements aimed at incapacitating an attacker.

Escuela de Cuchillo (Knife School): Colombia has a tradition of practical knife defense that incorporates local street fighting methods and influences from Spanish and indigenous practices. In recent years, this has led to more formalized self-defense training, especially in response to rising concerns about street violence.

Peru

Andean Knives and Kukuli: In Peru's Andean region, knives are part of daily life and traditional practices. Small knives called *kukuli* are often used for ritual and utility, serving both ceremonial and practical roles in indigenous communities.

The Machete in the Amazon: In the Peruvian Amazon, the machete is widely used for work and self-defense. For many indigenous communities, it is an essential tool for survival in the dense jungle, where it's used for tasks from food preparation to constructing shelters.

Martial Arts Influence: Knife techniques have begun to emerge in Peruvian martial arts, where instructors integrate traditional indigenous knife skills and machete handling into more modern self-defense systems.

Venezuela

Knives in Rural and Urban Life: In rural Venezuela, knives serve as essential tools for farmers and ranchers, used for everything from preparing food to managing livestock. The machete is especially important in rural communities, used both as a tool and as a means of self-defense.

Urban Knife Culture and Crime: In cities like Caracas, knives are frequently used in street altercations, both for defense and by criminal elements. Knife attacks are common in some high-crime areas, leading many Venezuelans to carry knives for personal protection.

Knife Defense Training: In response to the prevalence of knives in urban crime, self-defense schools in Venezuela now often include knife defense techniques in their curriculums, preparing students to respond to blade-based attacks.

Ecuador and Bolivia

Everyday Carry and Utility Knives: In both Ecuador and Bolivia, knives are common tools for rural and indigenous communities, where they serve agricultural and everyday purposes.

Machetes and Jungle Survival: In Ecuador's Amazonian regions, as in Peru, the machete is an essential survival tool for indigenous communities and local laborers.

Indigenous Knife Techniques: Some indigenous communities in Ecuador and Bolivia use traditional knives for hunting and ritual purposes. These knives are often designed for specific practical tasks and can vary greatly by region and indigenous group.

Influence of Knife Culture on Martial Arts and Self-Defense in South America

Throughout South America, there is growing interest in formalized knife training, especially for self-defense in urban areas where knife-related violence has become a concern. Many South American martial artists have adapted their knife techniques from both indigenous and imported methods, incorporating them into systems such as Brazilian Jiu-Jitsu, Capoeira, and other local arts.

Knife training schools that teach defense against blades are increasingly popular, often blending local knife-handling techniques with global combatives knowledge, creating systems that reflect the unique cultural contexts of South American countries.

Summary

Knife culture in South America is shaped by both practicality and necessity, with knives serving as symbols of heritage, tools of survival, and, in some cases, weapons for self-protection. These varied roles reflect the deep cultural significance of knives across the continent, as well as the enduring need for practical edged-weapon skills.

Scandinavia

Knife culture in Scandinavian countries is rich and deeply rooted, with knives valued as essential tools for survival, craftsmanship, and cultural heritage. Scandinavian knives are celebrated for their high-quality craftsmanship, functional designs, and simplicity, reflecting the region's connection to nature and practical lifestyle. Here's a look at knife culture in Norway, Sweden, Finland, and Denmark:

Norway

The Norwegian *Tollekniv*: The *tollekniv*, or "utility knife," is a traditional Norwegian knife used for a wide range of tasks, from wood carving to fishing and camping. Its simple, durable design typically includes a single, fixed blade with a sturdy wooden handle.

Outdoor and Survival Skills: With Norway's expansive wilderness, knives are essential for outdoor activities like hiking, hunting, and fishing. Norwegians, especially in rural areas, carry knives for practical use, whether they're making a campfire, preparing food, or carving wood.

Craftsmanship and Family Heirlooms: Knives often hold sentimental value in Norwegian families, with many people inheriting handmade knives that have been passed down through generations. The tradition of gifting knives is also common, particularly as a rite of passage or a personal milestone.

Traditional and Modern Brands: Helle is one of Norway's renowned knife manufacturers, producing high-quality knives that blend traditional craftsmanship with modern materials. These knives are popular among outdoor enthusiasts and collectors alike.

Sweden

The Morakniv: The *Morakniv*, a type of utility knife originating in the Mora region, is one of Sweden's most iconic knives. Known for its affordable price and robust design, the Morakniv is used for bushcraft, woodworking, and general outdoor tasks. It's popular worldwide for its simplicity, versatility, and reliability.

Woodworking and Carving: Swedish culture has a strong tradition of wood carving, and knives are essential for this craft. Many Swedes learn knife skills from an early age, practicing carving with Morakniv or other locally made knives. These skills are often passed down through families.

Bushcraft and Outdoor Culture: Knives are integral to Swedish bushcraft, which emphasizes self-sufficiency and survival skills in nature. Many Swedes carry fixed-blade knives for camping, fishing, and wilderness exploration, making these knives a vital part of their outdoor gear.

Brands Known for Quality: In addition to Morakniv, brands like EKA and Karesuando produce high-quality knives that cater to outdoor enthusiasts and collectors. Swedish knives are appreciated for their practicality, durability, and high-quality steel.

Finland

The Puukko: The *puukko* is perhaps Finland's most famous knife and a symbol of Finnish culture. With a simple, fixed blade and ergonomic handle, the puukko is versatile and used for a variety of tasks, from hunting and fishing to wood carving. It is so iconic that the puukko has come to represent Finnish resilience and craftsmanship.

Symbolic and Practical Value: In Finland, the puukko is not only a tool but also a symbol of pride and tradition. It is often given as a gift to mark significant life events, such as graduations, weddings, or the start of military service. Many Finns see the puukko as a cultural icon and a representation of Finnish "sisu," or resilience.

Marttiini Knives: Marttiini is one of Finland's most renowned knife manufacturers, producing traditional puukkos as well as other outdoor knives. The brand is known for its high-quality steel, functional design, and attention to detail, making Marttiini knives highly sought after both in Finland and internationally.

Everyday Utility and Bushcraft: The puukko is commonly carried by Finns who spend time in nature, where it's used for everything from cooking to carving. Finns also value bushcraft skills, and the puukko's design makes it ideal for survival tasks in Finland's challenging wilderness.

Denmark

The Snittekniv and Outdoor Knives: Although Denmark doesn't have a singular iconic knife like the puukko or Morakniv, traditional carving knives known as *snittekniv* are popular for wood carving and craft. These small, precise knives are used in whittling and other traditional crafts, especially among hobbyists.

Outdoor Utility: Danes who spend time outdoors, such as hikers, campers, and hunters, often carry fixed-blade knives for practical purposes. In the Danish countryside, knives are still widely used for camping, fishing, and everyday tasks.

Legal Restrictions and Utility Knives: Denmark has relatively strict knife laws, limiting public carry of locking and fixed-blade knives. As a result, most Danes who carry knives in urban settings use smaller folding knives for utility, within legal limits. In rural areas or outdoor settings, however, larger knives are more commonly used.

Emphasis on Functionality: Danish knife designs are often simple and functional, reflecting the Scandinavian ethos of minimalism and practicality. Danish brands such as Fällkniven (although Swedish-founded, widely used in Denmark) focus on high-quality, durable knives for both everyday use and outdoor survival.

Common Themes Across Scandinavian Knife Culture

High-Quality Craftsmanship: Scandinavian knives are known for their craftsmanship and functional design, with brands like Morakniv, Helle, and Marttiini producing knives that emphasize durability and simplicity. Scandinavian knife-making uses high-quality carbon and stainless steels that hold an edge well, making them ideal for outdoor tasks.

Outdoor and Survival Skills: Scandinavians have a deep respect for nature, and knife skills are essential for those engaging in activities like camping, hunting, and fishing. Knives are not only tools but integral parts of the Scandinavian approach to self-sufficiency, bushcraft, and wilderness survival.

Cultural and Symbolic Importance: Knives in Scandinavia hold cultural significance and are often viewed as symbols of heritage and resilience. The Finnish puukko, Norwegian tollekniv, and Swedish Morakniv are all symbols of national pride, reflecting the strength and craftsmanship valued in these societies.

Knife as a Rite of Passage: In many Scandinavian countries, children are introduced to knives at a young age, learning responsible use and respect for tools. Receiving a knife is often a rite of passage, and many families pass down knives as heirlooms, fostering a sense of tradition and continuity.

Legal Restrictions and Responsible Carry: Scandinavian countries generally have stricter regulations on carrying knives in public, particularly in urban areas. Knives are widely accepted as tools, especially in rural areas, but there is a strong emphasis on responsible use. Fixed-blade knives are preferred for outdoor activities, while small folding knives are common for everyday utility.

Influence on Global Knife Culture

Scandinavian knife designs, especially the puukko and Morakniv, have had a profound influence on global knife culture. Known for their reliability, simplicity, and ergonomic design, these knives are popular among bushcraft and survival enthusiasts worldwide. The Scandinavian grind—a type of blade grind that makes sharpening easy and effective—is widely used in knife-making and admired for its practicality in outdoor contexts.

Summary

Knife culture in Scandinavia is rooted in practicality, craftsmanship, and respect for tradition. Knives are seen as essential tools for outdoor life and self-sufficiency, valued not only for their utility but also for their cultural significance. Scandinavian knives reflect a blend of function and heritage, embodying the minimalist and resilient spirit of the Nordic region.

Western Europe

Knife culture in Western European countries is deeply influenced by historical traditions, utility, craftsmanship, and modern legal restrictions. While knives remain essential tools in rural and urban areas alike, they also hold cultural significance in many Western European societies. Let's explore knife culture in some Western European countries:

United Kingdom

Historical Fighting Knives: The UK has a historical tradition of fighting knives, such as the *sgian-dubh* (a small, ceremonial knife worn with traditional Scottish Highland dress) and the *dirk* (a long dagger used by Highland Scots). These knives are now symbolic, often reserved for ceremonial use.

Everyday Carry (EDC) and Legal Restrictions: The UK has strict knife laws, with prohibitions on carrying knives with blades longer than 3 inches (unless for work) and on carrying locking or fixed blades in public without a valid reason. Many British people carry small non-locking folding knives, often within legal limits, for tasks such as cutting or opening items.

Interest in Bushcraft and Outdoor Knives: The popularity of bushcraft and survival skills has led to a rise in knife use among enthusiasts. Many bushcraft knives are fixed blades with Scandinavian designs (e.g., Morakniv), and they're commonly used for outdoor skills like carving, fire-making, and food preparation.

Knife Collecting and Customization: Knife collecting and appreciation for traditional craftsmanship are prevalent in the UK, with some people collecting traditional folding knives and customized models. Collectors appreciate unique designs, historical replicas, and high-quality, custom-made knives, often following legal restrictions.

France

The Opinel and Laguiole Knives: France has a strong knife culture with a focus on craftsmanship and utility. Two iconic knives are the *Opinel* and *Laguiole*, both popular folding knives with simple, functional designs. Opinel knives are affordable and widely used for everyday tasks, while Laguiole knives are more decorative and are often handmade, serving as prized possessions and symbols of French craftsmanship.

Culinary Significance: In a country famous for its cuisine, knives hold a special place in French culture. Culinary knives, from paring to chef's knives, are integral to French cooking, and many people invest in high-quality kitchen knives from brands like Sabatier and Thiers-Issard. French chefs and home cooks alike value knives as essential tools.

Everyday Carry and Legal Restrictions: French knife laws allow folding knives for EDC, but restrictions prohibit carrying them in certain public spaces, especially those designed for self-defense or with aggressive designs. While knives are commonly used tools, carrying one in urban areas can draw scrutiny.

Collecting and Artisanal Knives: France has a long tradition of artisanal knife-making, especially in regions like Thiers, known as the country's knife capital. Many knife collectors prize hand-crafted French knives for their quality, and they're often passed down as family heirlooms.

Germany

Practicality and Precision in Knife Use: German knife culture emphasizes precision and utility, with knives seen as practical tools in both everyday life and outdoor activities. German craftsmanship is highly respected, with brands like Wüsthof, Zwilling, and Boker producing knives that are valued worldwide for quality and durability.

The Influence of Solingen: The city of Solingen is a historical hub for knife and blade manufacturing in Germany, known as the "City of Blades." It has a long-standing reputation for producing high-quality knives, including utility knives, swords, and kitchen knives. Solingen-made knives are regarded as symbols of German engineering and craftsmanship.

Strict Legal Regulations: Germany has strict knife laws, prohibiting automatic knives, certain types of folding knives, and long-bladed knives in public. Germans who carry knives for utility often choose smaller, folding pocket knives that comply with the law.

Interest in Bushcraft and Outdoor Skills: Many Germans are drawn to outdoor activities, and bushcraft knives are popular among enthusiasts who enjoy camping, hiking, and survival skills. These knives are typically fixed blades with sturdy construction, used for wood carving, food preparation, and other outdoor tasks.

Switzerland

The Swiss Army Knife: The Swiss Army Knife, produced by Victorinox and Wenger, is one of Switzerland's most famous cultural icons. Known for its versatility and compact design, the Swiss Army Knife is a popular EDC tool worldwide. In Switzerland, it's widely used for practical purposes, from hiking to household tasks.

Craftsmanship and Quality: Swiss craftsmanship is highly regarded, with Victorinox producing various types of knives, including culinary knives. The Swiss Army Knife represents Swiss values of practicality, durability, and innovation.

EDC and Legal Considerations: Switzerland has some restrictions on knife carrying, particularly regarding locking blades and larger knives. However, the Swiss Army Knife is generally acceptable and commonly carried by many Swiss people for its practical utility.

Outdoor and Survival Skills: Swiss people enjoy outdoor activities such as hiking and mountaineering, and knives play a role in their outdoor culture. The versatility of the Swiss Army Knife makes it a staple for Swiss outdoorsmen, and it's seen as a reliable tool for emergencies and survival.

Italy

Historical Folding Knives: Italy has a rich tradition of folding knives, particularly from the regions of Sardinia and Sicily. The *resolza* from Sardinia and the *navaja* from Sicily are popular folding knives with distinctive designs, historically carried by farmers and shepherds for daily tasks and personal protection.

Knife Craftsmanship: Italian knives, such as those made in Maniago (the "knife capital" of Italy), are known for their quality and artisanal craftsmanship. Many Italians appreciate finely made knives, especially those with intricate designs, and value them as collectibles or heirlooms.

Kitchen Knives and Culinary Culture: Italian cooking culture places a high value on quality kitchen knives, used by both chefs and home cooks. Italian brands like LionSteel and FOX produce high-quality kitchen and folding knives, which are both functional and aesthetic.

Legal Regulations and EDC: Italian knife laws are strict, with restrictions on carrying knives in public. Many Italians carry folding knives with short blades that are suitable for everyday tasks but comply with regulations. Knives with historical or decorative value are often reserved for home use or special occasions.

Spain

The Navaja: The *navaja*, a traditional folding knife, is an iconic symbol in Spain. Originally used by Andalusian shepherds and farmers, it became associated with dueling and self-defense. Today, the navaja is valued for its craftsmanship and is commonly used as a utility tool or collected as a piece of Spanish heritage.

Craftsmanship in Albacete: Albacete is Spain's traditional knife-making center, where craftsmen produce a variety of knives, including folding navajas and high-quality culinary knives. The city is known for its artisan knife makers, who produce both functional and decorative knives, often showcasing intricate detailing and unique handle designs.

Culinary Knives and Gastronomy: Spanish gastronomy relies heavily on quality kitchen knives for preparing foods like jamón (ham) and seafood. Specialized knives are used to slice jamón, and brands like Arcos produce high-quality chef's knives that are staples in Spanish kitchens.

Knife Regulations: Spain has strict laws regarding knife carrying in public, especially in urban areas. Spaniards often carry small, non-locking folding knives for utility, while larger or traditional knives are reserved for specific tasks or collected for historical significance.

Greece

The Kopis: Greece's knife culture is intertwined with its deep history, reaching back to ancient times when blades like the *kopis* and *xiphos* were integral to the hoplite warriors. These ancient weapons, used for slashing and thrusting in battle, were forged with practicality and power in mind. While the kopis is now more of a historical reference, its influence can be seen in the robust knives still used in rural Greece, where blades serve as essential tools for shepherds and farmers. The Cretan *sfakian dagger*, a more modern emblem of Greek knife tradition, is steeped in symbolism and is often passed down as an heirloom or worn during cultural events.

Craftsmanship: Greek knife craftsmanship has long been a blend of functionality and artistry. In Crete, skilled artisans continue to hand-forge blades with fine engravings and handle designs that incorporate bone, horn, or wood, reflecting the island's heritage and spirit of independence. Each knife is made with meticulous attention to detail, and local craftsmen take pride in techniques passed down through generations, often combining traditional methods with modern innovations to maintain the quality and prestige of Greek blades.

Regulations: Regulations surrounding knives in Greece are relatively strict, particularly in urban areas where carrying knives without a valid reason is prohibited. The laws aim to prevent violence and restrict the carrying of any blade that could be used as a weapon. However, rural communities where knives are considered essential for daily activities have more relaxed enforcement, acknowledging the cultural and practical importance of knives in agricultural life. Collectors and enthusiasts can still acquire traditional knives, but they must adhere to guidelines regarding transportation and display.

Common Themes Across Western Europe

Craftsmanship and Tradition: Western Europe is known for its high-quality knife craftsmanship, with each country having its own iconic knife designs and renowned production centers, such as Solingen in Germany, Thiers in France, and Albacete in Spain. These regions emphasize the artistry of knife-making, and many knives are valued for their craftsmanship as much as their function.

Regulation and Restriction: Knife laws are generally strict across Western Europe, particularly in urban areas. Most countries prohibit carrying knives for self-defense, and there are restrictions on blade length, locking mechanisms, and types of knives. As a result, Europeans tend to carry small folding knives for utility rather than self-defense.

Utility and Outdoor Culture: Many Western Europeans carry knives for practical uses, such as cooking, gardening, and outdoor activities. Bushcraft and outdoor knives are popular among enthusiasts, with fixed-blade knives being used in camping and survival contexts. These knives reflect a respect for craftsmanship and the practicality of being prepared in natural settings.

Culinary Significance: With rich culinary traditions, Western Europe places a high value on quality kitchen knives. Knives are essential tools in professional and home kitchens, and there is an appreciation for finely made culinary knives. Brands such as Wüsthof, Zwilling, and

Victorinox are well-regarded for their quality and durability in food preparation.

Summary

Knife culture in Western Europe reflects a balance of practicality, respect for craftsmanship, and compliance with strict regulations. Knives are appreciated both as tools and as expressions of cultural heritage, with a focus on utility and skill rather than as weapons for self-defense.

Eastern Europe

Knife culture in Eastern European countries has evolved through a mix of historical significance, regional craftsmanship, practical utility, and, in some cases, defensive use. The region's knife culture reflects diverse influences, from traditional weaponry to rural life and contemporary knife-making. Here's a look at knife culture across several Eastern European countries:

Russia

The Traditional Finnish Puukko and Soviet Influence: In northern Russia, close to Finland, the *puukko* (a small, versatile knife) is widely used as a utility tool. Russia has adapted this design, producing similar knives for hunting, woodworking, and survival.

The Kindjal: The *kindjal*, a double-edged dagger with origins in the Caucasus region, has a storied history in Russia. Though largely ceremonial today, it remains a symbol of heritage and is admired for its craftsmanship.

Soviet-Era Military Knives: Knives like the *NR-40* were standard-issue for Soviet soldiers and remain iconic in Russian military history. Many Russians respect military-grade knives for their durability, and some collect them as historical artifacts.

Outdoor and Survival Culture: Russians highly value knives for outdoor activities, with knives commonly used in hunting, fishing, and camping. Fixed-blade knives are popular among those who enjoy bushcraft and wilderness survival in the vast Russian countryside.

Poland

Traditional Folding Knives and Scout Culture: Polish folding knives, especially among scouts and outdoor enthusiasts, are popular for their practicality and accessibility. The *scyzoryk* (a folding knife) is a well-known knife type in Poland and is often used for camping, hunting, and everyday tasks.

Military Influence: Polish military knives, such as the *wz.55*, are highly regarded among collectors and enthusiasts. Many Polish people have an interest in knives with military heritage, appreciating them as functional tools and pieces of national history.

Rural and Agricultural Use: In rural Poland, fixed-blade knives are used for agricultural tasks, animal processing, and wood carving. Traditional knife-making in regions like Podhale preserves local designs that are both practical and culturally significant.

Czech Republic and Slovakia

Traditional Craftsmanship: In both the Czech Republic and Slovakia, traditional knives are crafted by local artisans, especially in regions like Mikulášovice (Czech Republic), known as a center for knife-making. These knives are prized for their quality and often have unique, regionally inspired designs.

Hunting and Outdoor Culture: Hunting is popular in both countries, and hunting knives are highly valued for their functionality. Fixed-blade knives are commonly used by hunters and outdoorsmen for field dressing, camping, and bushcraft.

Everyday Carry and Legal Restrictions: Czech and Slovak laws are relatively lenient on knife carry compared to other parts of Europe. Folding knives are commonly carried for practical use, especially by rural residents and outdoor enthusiasts, who use them for everything from food preparation to repair tasks.

Hungary

Traditional Knives (Fokos and Bicska): The *fokos* is a traditional Hungarian axe-knife hybrid historically used by shepherds, while the *bicska* is a folding knife commonly carried by Hungarians for utility tasks. Both are symbols of Hungarian heritage and are appreciated for their functional designs.

Agricultural and Shepherd Use: Rural Hungary has a strong tradition of using knives and small tools for agricultural and shepherding purposes. Farmers and herders often carry folding or fixed-blade knives for everyday tasks and animal processing.

Culinary Influence: In Hungary's rich culinary culture, high-quality kitchen knives are appreciated for food preparation, particularly for traditional dishes involving meat. Hungarian households often invest in well-made kitchen knives for their durability and effectiveness.

Romania

The Briceag and Traditional Knives: The *briceag*, a small folding knife, is popular in Romania, especially in rural areas where it's used for farming, gardening, and food preparation. Traditional fixed-blade knives are also used in rural life, with designs passed down through generations.

Knives in Folklore and Symbolism: Knives have a place in Romanian folklore, symbolizing protection, strength, and self-reliance. The use of knives in Romanian tradition is deeply rooted in rural culture, where they were seen as essential tools and symbols of resourcefulness.

Outdoor and Bushcraft Interest: Romania's natural landscapes encourage outdoor activities, and knives are commonly used for camping, hunting, and hiking. Bushcraft knives and fixed blades are particularly popular among Romanians interested in outdoor survival skills.

Ukraine

Traditional Cossack Blades: The Cossacks of Ukraine used distinctive blades, such as the *shashka* (a curved sword) and various knives for combat and survival. Though the shashka is largely ceremonial today, it remains an important cultural symbol.

Self-Reliance and Rural Knife Use: In rural areas, knives are practical tools for farming and animal processing. Many Ukrainians carry folding or fixed-blade knives for everyday tasks, particularly in agricultural communities where knives are essential for working the land.

Military Knives and Tactical Interest: Given Ukraine's recent history of conflict, there has been a resurgence of interest in tactical and military knives. Many Ukrainians respect military knives for their durability and functionality, with some collecting them as symbols of resilience.

Bulgaria

Traditional Folding Knives: The *nozh* is a traditional Bulgarian folding knife, often carried by men for utility purposes. These knives are highly regarded for their simplicity and effectiveness and are commonly used in rural and agricultural areas.

Rural Utility and Everyday Carry: In Bulgaria's rural areas, knives are widely used for agricultural tasks, woodworking, and food preparation. Many Bulgarians carry small folding knives for practical purposes, particularly those living in farming communities.

Cultural Significance: Knives in Bulgaria hold cultural value, particularly among rural and mountain communities. They are often seen as symbols of self-reliance and are given as gifts or handed down as heirlooms within families.

Common Themes Across Eastern Europe

Historical and Cultural Significance: Many Eastern European countries have traditional knife designs that are tied to regional identity and heritage, such as the kindjal in Russia, the fokos in Hungary, and the Cossack blades in Ukraine. These knives are often seen as symbols of pride, resilience, and craftsmanship.

Practical Utility in Rural Life: Knives are essential tools in Eastern Europe, especially in rural areas where they are used for farming, animal processing, woodworking, and food preparation. People in rural Eastern Europe often carry folding or fixed-blade knives for practical daily tasks.

Military Influence: Military knives and tactical blades are respected across Eastern Europe, with many people valuing the strength and durability of knives designed for combat. Military and survival knives are often collected by enthusiasts and valued for their connection to national history.

Outdoor and Bushcraft Culture: Eastern Europe's natural landscapes encourage outdoor activities, and knives play a key role in bushcraft, hunting, and camping. People interested in survival skills often favor durable, fixed-blade knives that can withstand rugged use in wilderness settings.

Martial Arts and Self-Defense Training: Knife-based martial arts, particularly those originating in Russia, like *Systema*, include knife defense and usage. In regions where street violence may be a concern, informal knife fighting techniques have emerged, emphasizing practical self-defense tactics.

Legal Restrictions and Everyday Carry

Many Eastern European countries have relatively relaxed knife laws, especially for folding knives and knives carried for utility rather than self-defense. Restrictions do exist for certain blade types or lengths in urban areas, but knives are widely accepted in rural settings.

Knives are commonly carried in Eastern Europe, especially in rural areas, where they are viewed as necessary tools rather than weapons. In urban areas, smaller folding knives are generally acceptable for everyday carry, while larger or tactical knives are more likely to face scrutiny.

Summary

Knife culture in Eastern Europe combines a strong sense of heritage, utility, and practicality. Knives are valued as both tools and symbols, and their use is tied to the region's rural traditions, outdoor lifestyle, and martial history. Despite varying levels of regulation, knives remain an integral part of daily life and cultural identity in Eastern European countries.

Middle East

Knife culture in Middle Eastern countries is steeped in tradition, craftsmanship, and symbolism. Knives in the Middle East are valued for their practical uses, historical significance, and cultural identity, often reflecting the region's diverse history and intricate artisan skills. Many Middle Eastern knives also hold ceremonial or symbolic roles, connected to cultural identity, religious traditions, and martial heritage. Here's an exploration of knife culture across several Middle Eastern countries:

Saudi Arabia

The Jambiya: The *jambiya*, a traditional curved dagger with a distinctive hilt, is an iconic symbol in Saudi Arabia, particularly in the southwestern Asir region. Worn as part of traditional dress, it is often an indicator of social status and heritage. A jambiya is usually worn by men during festivals, weddings, and other significant cultural events.

Cultural Significance: Jambiyas are often elaborately decorated with silver or gold, and the handle may be made from horn, wood, or ivory, indicating the owner's social rank. Passing down a jambiya from father to son is a tradition in many families, making it a symbol of continuity and honor.

Utility and Ceremonial Use: Though primarily symbolic, jambiyas have historically been used for protection and as tools. In modern Saudi Arabia, however, they are mostly ceremonial and rarely used in a practical capacity.

Yemen

The Yemeni Jambiya: In Yemen, the jambiya holds significant cultural value. Yemeni men wear it as part of their everyday attire, and it is often displayed prominently across the belt. The blade is usually double-edged and has a curved design, with a handle often crafted from valuable materials like rhino horn or silver.

Social Symbol and Rite of Passage: The jambiya symbolizes manhood and social status in Yemeni culture, with young boys receiving their first jambiya as a rite of passage into adulthood. It is also a mark of identity, often reflecting the region and tribe to which the wearer belongs.

Craftsmanship and Symbolism: Yemeni jambiyas are known for their intricate craftsmanship. Skilled artisans produce ornate scabbards and handles, and certain designs signify regional identity or tribal affiliation, with each style carrying its unique heritage.

Oman

The Khanjar: The *khanjar*, a curved dagger similar to the jambiya, is a prominent cultural symbol in Oman. It is traditionally worn by men on ceremonial occasions and is even featured on Oman's national emblem. Omani khanjars are unique for their ornate, often silver-inlaid scabbards and hilts, which represent regional craftsmanship.

Status Symbol and Heritage: Owning a finely crafted khanjar is a mark of prestige in Omani society, and the quality and decoration of the dagger can signify the wealth or social standing of the wearer. Many khanjars are passed down as family heirlooms, preserving family history and traditions.

Ceremonial Use and Modern Pride: While khanjars were once practical weapons, they are now largely ceremonial. However, they retain deep cultural significance, and Omani men often wear them during national celebrations, weddings, and religious festivals as symbols of pride and heritage.

United Arab Emirates (UAE)

The Khanjar in the UAE: Like Oman, the UAE also has a tradition of the khanjar, which holds similar cultural importance as a ceremonial dagger worn by men. In the UAE, khanjars are often crafted with silver filigree and decorated with intricate designs that reflect Emirati heritage.

Symbol of Heritage and National Identity: The khanjar in the UAE is associated with Bedouin culture and is a symbol of national identity. Emirati men wear the khanjar on formal occasions as a mark of tradition and respect for their ancestors.

Contemporary Significance: The khanjar has become a patriotic symbol in the UAE and is featured in Emirati art and souvenirs. It is also worn by Emirati officials and leaders during national events, reinforcing its role as a cultural icon.

Iran

The Kard and Qame: Iran has a rich tradition of knife and sword making, with distinctive styles like the *kard* (a straight-bladed knife) and *qame* (a short, broad dagger). Historically, these knives were used for both utility and self-defense, especially in rural and tribal regions.

Artisan Craftsmanship: Persian knives and daggers are often intricately decorated, with handles and scabbards featuring elaborate carvings, calligraphy, and precious inlays. Iranian craftsmen are known for producing high-quality steel blades with beautiful engravings.

Ceremonial and Collectible Knives: In modern Iran, traditional knives like the kard and qame are valued as collector's items and decorative pieces rather than practical tools. They are often displayed in homes or used in ceremonies, symbolizing the country's long-standing artisan heritage.

Turkey

The Yatagan and Sykes Dagger: The *yatagan*, a curved knife that resembles a short sword, has historical roots in Turkey. Originally used by Ottoman soldiers, it is now a symbol of Turkish heritage and martial history. The Sykes dagger, a double-edged knife developed during WWII, also has a Turkish version popular among collectors and reenactors.

Knives in Everyday Life: In rural Turkey, smaller knives are still widely used for agricultural tasks and daily work. Shepherds, farmers, and craftsmen rely on utility knives for practical purposes.

Culinary Knives and Traditional Cuisine: Turkish cuisine values quality kitchen knives, especially for meat preparation and vegetable cutting. Turkish butchers and chefs often use specialized knives for traditional dishes, and many Turkish households invest in well-made kitchen knives as essentials for cooking.

Lebanon and Syria

Historical Dagger Styles: Lebanon and Syria have a history of producing beautifully crafted daggers with styles that resemble the khanjar or jambiya but feature unique local variations. These knives often have curved blades with decorated handles, reflecting the region's artisan skills.

Utility and Heritage: In rural areas of Lebanon and Syria, small folding knives are common for practical tasks. Knives are essential tools for farmers and craftsmen, used in everything from agriculture to carpentry.

Symbolism and Decorative Use: Traditionally crafted knives are popular collectibles in Lebanon and Syria, appreciated for their historical significance and detailed ornamentation. These knives are often displayed in homes as symbols of pride in local craftsmanship and heritage.

Israel

Utility and Tactical Knives: In Israel, knives are commonly used in military and security contexts, with tactical knives being part of standard gear for soldiers in the Israel Defense Forces (IDF). Brands like "Nimrod" have produced tactical knives specifically for IDF use, and these knives are highly regarded for their durability and utility.

Everyday Carry and Self-Defense: Given security concerns, some Israelis carry folding or fixed-blade knives for self-defense. Knife training and self-defense techniques are part of krav maga, Israel's martial art, where practitioners learn to defend against and handle knives.

Culinary and Cultural Significance: Israeli cuisine values high-quality kitchen knives, especially for preparing dishes that involve precision cuts, like kebabs and vegetables. Quality knives are appreciated for their role in preparing traditional foods, reflecting Israel's diverse culinary heritage.

Common Themes Across Middle Eastern Knife Culture

Symbolism and Status: Knives like the khanjar and jambiya hold immense cultural value as symbols of social status, masculinity, and heritage. These knives are often given as gifts and passed down through generations, symbolizing honor and tradition.

Artisan Craftsmanship: Middle Eastern knives are renowned for their detailed craftsmanship. Artisans use silver, gold, and precious stones to adorn handles and scabbards, creating knives that are as much works of art as functional tools. Each region's knife design reflects local materials, artistry, and traditions.

Ceremonial and Decorative Use: While knives were once essential tools and weapons, many traditional Middle Eastern knives are now used primarily for ceremonial and decorative purposes. Men wear these knives at weddings, festivals, and national events to showcase cultural pride and respect for tradition.

Utility in Rural Life: In rural areas, knives are still essential tools for farming, shepherding, and hunting. Practical knives are widely used across the region for daily tasks, from cooking to agriculture, and they are valued for their functionality.

Military and Tactical Use: In certain Middle Eastern countries, knives are also part of military or security equipment, with tactical knives issued to soldiers and law enforcement personnel. Knife handling and defense are components of military training in Israel and other areas, with knives seen as essential for close-quarters situations.

Influence on Global Knife Culture

Middle Eastern knife designs, such as the khanjar and jambiya, have influenced global knife-making and are appreciated by collectors and martial artists worldwide. Middle Eastern craftsmanship, known for its attention to detail, has contributed to a high standard in decorative knife-making, inspiring artisans globally to incorporate traditional Middle Eastern motifs and techniques into their designs.

Summary

Knife culture in the Middle East is a blend of functionality, artistry, and cultural symbolism. Knives like the khanjar, jambiya, and yatagan are deeply embedded in Middle Eastern identity, representing a heritage of craftsmanship, social status, and traditional values. While many of these knives are now primarily ceremonial, they continue to be cherished for their historical and cultural significance.

Central Asia

Knife culture in Central Asian countries is deeply rooted in the region's nomadic history, tribal traditions, and practical, everyday uses. Knives are essential tools for survival, craftsmanship, and cultural expression. Many knives in Central Asia are known for their distinctive designs, often combining functionality with artistic decoration, and they hold symbolic value within various communities. Here's a look at knife culture across several Central Asian countries:

Kazakhstan

The Bichak and Pchak: Traditional Kazakh knives, such as the *bichak* and *pchak*, are used for various daily tasks, including food preparation, animal processing, and general utility work. These knives often have wide, single-edged blades with handles made from wood or horn.

Nomadic Heritage and Practical Use: Kazakhstan's nomadic past has greatly influenced its knife culture. For Kazakh herders and rural dwellers, knives are essential tools used in hunting, livestock care, and setting up camp. The knives are often kept simple but are made to withstand the demands of nomadic life.

Ceremonial and Symbolic Significance: Some knives are intricately decorated and hold ceremonial value, symbolizing strength, self-reliance, and heritage. Men often pass knives down through generations, and giving a knife as a gift can be a sign of respect and good fortune.

Craftsmanship and Aesthetics: Kazakh knives are often hand-forged by local artisans, who decorate them with traditional engravings. Handles are crafted from materials like bone or antler, and the scabbards may feature traditional patterns, blending artistry with utility.

Uzbekistan

The Pchak: The *pchak* is one of Uzbekistan's most iconic knives, widely used in daily life, particularly in the kitchen. Known for its slightly curved, wide blade, the pchak is highly valued for its ability to handle a variety of tasks, from chopping vegetables to cutting meat.

Culinary Importance: Uzbeks use the pchak extensively in their cuisine, especially for preparing dishes like *plov* (pilaf) and kebabs. A well-crafted pchak is prized in Uzbek kitchens, and the skill of preparing food with it is often considered a mark of a good cook.

Distinctive Craftsmanship: The city of Bukhara is famous for its pchak knives, known for their high-quality blades and decorated handles. Uzbek artisans decorate pchak knives with intricate patterns and inlaid handles, often using materials like bone, wood, and horn. The knives are frequently adorned with bright colors and geometric designs, making them both functional and artistic.

Gift and Symbolic Use: In Uzbekistan, pchak knives are often given as gifts to signify respect, hospitality, or goodwill. A beautifully crafted pchak can serve as a family heirloom, passed down across generations.

Turkmenistan

The Traditional Knife (Kord): In Turkmenistan, knives like the *kord* are common, used as practical tools by both rural and urban populations. These knives are typically long, single-edged, and designed for versatility, often resembling a short sword or large dagger.

Craftsmanship and Decoration: Turkmen knives are often decorated with traditional motifs, and the handles may be inlaid with silver, ivory, or mother-of-pearl. Knife artisans pay great attention to detail, ensuring that the knives are both functional and visually appealing.

Symbol of Protection and Wealth: Knives in Turkmen culture are sometimes viewed as talismans for protection and symbols of wealth. Many families keep decorative knives at home or display them as part of traditional attire, particularly during ceremonies or national events.

Utility in Pastoral Life: For Turkmen herders and rural communities, knives are vital for tasks related to livestock care and camping. The knife is essential in the daily life of shepherds, and many Turkmen grow up learning knife-handling skills as part of their pastoral heritage.

Tajikistan

Traditional Bolo Knives: The *bolo* knife, with its slightly curved blade, is popular in Tajikistan, used for agricultural and hunting tasks. These knives are practical, often featuring a wide blade suited to heavy-duty work.

Connection to Nomadic and Rural Life: In rural Tajikistan, knives are indispensable tools used for farming, preparing food, and maintaining livestock. Traditional knives are often straightforward in design but valued for their reliability and strength.

Gift and Cultural Significance: Giving a knife as a gift in Tajik culture is a common practice, symbolizing friendship, respect, and goodwill. Beautifully crafted knives are valued possessions and are often displayed in homes as symbols of tradition and skill.

Knife Craftsmanship: Tajik artisans craft knives that blend practicality with aesthetic appeal. Handles are frequently made from bone or wood, and the blades are often etched with traditional patterns. These knives are appreciated as symbols of Tajik craftsmanship and are valued in both everyday life and as collectible items.

Kyrgyzstan

The Bichak: The *bichak* is a traditional Kyrgyz knife, used for various tasks such as animal butchering, food preparation, and utility purposes. Its design is similar to the Uzbek pchak but may vary in blade shape and handle decoration depending on the region.

Essential Tool for Nomadic Life: Given Kyrgyzstan's strong nomadic heritage, knives are highly valued as survival tools. Many Kyrgyz people carry a knife daily, especially in rural and mountainous areas where they are used for herding, hunting, and camping.

Cultural Significance and Heritage: The knife holds a place of respect in Kyrgyz culture, often seen as a symbol of independence and self-reliance. Some knives are passed down as family heirlooms, connecting generations and preserving cultural traditions.

Craftsmanship and Ornate Decoration: Kyrgyz knives are often handmade, featuring decorated handles and scabbards. Artisans in Kyrgyzstan are skilled in adding intricate details, with designs that reflect Kyrgyz patterns and symbols. These knives are both functional and artistic, reflecting the craftsmanship and heritage of the region.

Afghanistan

The Khyber Knife: The *Khyber knife*, or *chura*, is a large, straight-bladed knife that originates from the Khyber Pass region, close to Afghanistan. Known for its strength and effectiveness, this knife has historically been used for combat and is a symbol of the warrior spirit in Afghan culture.

Functionality in Rural Life: In rural Afghan areas, knives are essential tools used for farming, cooking, and animal care. Many Afghans carry smaller knives or folding blades for daily utility tasks, particularly in tribal regions where traditional skills are highly valued.

Craftsmanship and Cultural Value: Afghan knives, particularly the Khyber knife, are often hand-forged and decorated with intricate engravings on the blade and handle. Craftsmen take pride in their work, and knives are appreciated for both their practical use and cultural symbolism.

Symbol of Tribal Identity and Defense: The Khyber knife is also a symbol of tribal identity, often associated with Pashtun culture. It is traditionally viewed as a tool for protection and a mark of personal and familial honor. Many Afghan families display these knives at home as symbols of heritage.

Common Themes Across Central Asian Knife Culture

Practical Use in Daily Life: In Central Asia, knives are practical tools essential for daily tasks, especially in rural and nomadic communities. They are used for cooking, herding, hunting, and other survival needs, reflecting the self-sufficient lifestyle of Central Asia's people.

Symbolism and Cultural Significance: Knives in Central Asia are often more than tools; they are symbols of heritage, identity, and masculinity. Receiving a knife can be a rite of passage or a sign of respect, and many knives are passed down through generations as family heirlooms.

Craftsmanship and Aesthetics: Central Asian knives are known for their intricate craftsmanship. Artisans decorate knives with traditional patterns, often inlaid with bone, horn, or metals like silver. This attention to detail makes Central Asian knives highly valued, both for their beauty and functionality.

Regional Variation and Identity: Each country or region in Central Asia has its own distinctive knife styles, such as the pchak in Uzbekistan and the Khyber knife in Afghanistan. These styles often signify regional and tribal identity, with specific designs reflecting local customs and history.

Gift and Honor Tradition: Gifting knives is a common practice in Central Asia, often symbolizing friendship, honor, and goodwill. A well-crafted knife is a respected gift, and its presentation is often associated with positive wishes for strength, resilience, and protection.

Influence on Global Knife Culture

Central Asian knives, such as the pchak and Khyber knife, are admired by collectors and martial artists worldwide for their craftsmanship and historical value. The unique designs and high-quality steel make these knives sought-after items in the global knife community, with many enthusiasts appreciating them for their practicality and cultural significance.

Summary

Knife culture in Central Asia reflects the region's nomadic history, practicality, and artistic heritage. Knives are seen as essential tools, symbols of honor, and works of art, representing the skills, resilience, and traditions of Central Asian people. Whether used in daily tasks or as ceremonial items, knives remain integral to the cultural identity and lifestyle of Central Asia.

South Asia

Knife culture in South Asian countries is rich, diverse, and deeply tied to the region's history, martial traditions, religious symbolism, and practical needs. Knives serve a range of purposes, from daily utility to martial arts and ceremonial practices, and many knives from South Asia are globally recognized for their unique designs and cultural significance. Here's an overview of knife culture across various South Asian countries:

India

The Kukri: Though primarily associated with Nepal, the *kukri* is also popular in northern India, especially among the Gorkha community and the Indian military. The kukri's curved blade and balance make it a versatile tool and weapon, used for chopping, combat, and ceremonial purposes.

The Bichwa and Katar: The *bichwa* (meaning "scorpion") and *katar* (push dagger) are traditional Indian knives that have been used historically in martial arts and warfare, particularly in Rajput and Maratha cultures. The katar's unique horizontal grip and double-edged blade were designed for piercing armor, while the bichwa's curved blade is associated with stealth and quick strikes.

Martial Arts and Kalari Weapons: Indian martial arts, such as *Kalaripayattu* in Kerala, incorporate knives as part of their traditional weaponry. The *urumi* (flexible sword), *vettuva val* (curved knife), and other blades are integral to training, and these weapons hold significant cultural and historical value.

Utility and Ritual Knives: Knives are essential in Indian rural and agricultural life, used for farming, cutting, and kitchen tasks. In some Hindu ceremonies, knives or small daggers are used for rituals and are believed to have protective powers. Knives are also used in the preparation of traditional dishes, and many Indian households own specialized kitchen knives.

Nepal

The Kukri: The *kukri* is a national symbol of Nepal and one of the most iconic knives in the world. Used by the Gurkhas, a renowned group of soldiers known for their bravery and skill, the kukri is both a weapon and a multipurpose tool for everyday tasks such as chopping wood and food preparation.

Cultural and Ceremonial Significance: In Nepali culture, the kukri is often given as a gift and is used in important life events. It symbolizes honor, courage, and loyalty, especially within the Gurkha community. The kukri also plays a role in religious ceremonies and sacrifices, especially during the festival of Dashain.

Craftsmanship and Heritage: Nepali artisans are skilled in kukri-making, often using high-quality steel to craft blades that are both functional and durable. The handles are traditionally made from wood, buffalo horn, or bone, with decorations that reflect Nepali artistry. Many families pass down kukris as heirlooms, adding to their cultural value.

Pakistan

The Pesh-Kabz and Choora: The *pesh-kabz* is a traditional dagger with a thick, reinforced blade, designed for penetrating armor. It originated in the Persian region and became popular in Pakistan and Afghanistan. The *choora* is another traditional knife, primarily used by Pashtun tribes in the northwest. Known for its straight, single-edged blade, the choora is used for both combat and practical tasks.

Utility and Rural Life: In rural Pakistan, knives are indispensable tools used for agriculture, hunting, and personal defense. The importance of knives is particularly pronounced in tribal areas, where they are symbols of pride and protection, often carried as part of traditional attire.

Artisan Craftsmanship: Pakistani knives, especially in cities like Peshawar, are renowned for their craftsmanship. Handles are often decorated with intricate carvings, inlays, and materials such as wood, bone, and ivory. These knives are both functional and collectible, valued for their strength and aesthetic appeal.

Knife Fighting in Martial Arts: Traditional Pakistani martial arts, like *Gatka*, include knife techniques, and many practitioners train with knives for self-defense and skill-building. Knives are also significant in Pakistan's military culture, with soldiers often carrying high-quality blades as part of their kit.

Sri Lanka

The Kastane: The *kastane* is a traditional Sri Lankan short sword, distinguished by its elaborate hilt with intricate lion and dragon motifs. Though it is more of a sword than a knife, the kastane holds cultural significance as a symbol of Sri Lankan heritage and is often seen in ceremonies and traditional displays.

Utility Knives in Rural Life: In rural Sri Lanka, smaller knives and machete-like tools are commonly used for farming, harvesting, and food preparation. Many Sri

Lankans carry utility knives to cut through dense vegetation, reflecting the knife's role in daily life.

Artistic and Ceremonial Value: Sri Lankan knives, especially the kastane, are valued for their intricate designs. These knives are crafted by skilled artisans, with handles often featuring detailed carvings and traditional symbols. Kastane swords are typically displayed in homes and used in ceremonial contexts, symbolizing bravery and heritage.

Bangladesh

The Dao: The *dao* is a large machete-like knife used in Bangladesh, particularly among hill tribes in the Chittagong Hill Tracts. It has a broad, single-edged blade and is used for cutting vegetation, hunting, and self-defense. The dao is highly versatile and serves as both a weapon and an everyday tool.

Ritual Knives and Ceremonial Use: In certain Bangladeshi communities, knives are used in rituals and ceremonies, often symbolizing strength or protection. Some ethnic groups incorporate knives into religious ceremonies and festivals, honoring them as sacred tools.

Importance in Rural Life: Knives are essential in Bangladeshi rural life, where they are used for fishing, farming, and household tasks. The *boti*, a traditional Bengali cutting tool with a curved blade mounted on a wooden base, is widely used in households for food preparation, especially in preparing fish, which is a staple of Bengali cuisine.

Artisan Craftsmanship: Bangladeshi knives, especially those made by hill tribes, often have handles decorated with carvings and colors unique to the tribal culture.

Craftsmanship is highly respected, and a well-made knife is seen as a sign of skill and pride.

Bhutan

The Traditional Knife (Dozum): Bhutanese people often carry a *dozum*, a traditional knife with a single-edged blade. The knife is practical and used for everyday tasks such as cutting wood, food preparation, and minor repairs. Bhutanese farmers and herders rely on the dozum for a range of tasks in rural areas.

Ritual and Cultural Symbolism: Knives in Bhutan are often used in religious rituals and are considered protective tools, symbolizing the ability to cut through obstacles or negativity. Some knives are even blessed by monks, reflecting their spiritual importance in Bhutanese culture.

Craftsmanship and Heirlooms: Bhutanese knives are often decorated with traditional motifs and may include intricate wood or metalwork. Many families pass knives down through generations, and they are treated with respect and reverence.

Common Themes Across South Asian Knife Culture

Practical Utility: Across South Asia, knives are essential tools for daily life, used in agriculture, food preparation, hunting, and self-defense. They are especially important in rural and tribal communities where traditional skills and self-sufficiency are valued.

Martial and Ceremonial Value: Knives and daggers hold historical and martial significance, with many types associated with warrior cultures, such as the kukri in Nepal and the pesh-kabz in Pakistan. In addition, knives are often used in religious and cultural ceremonies, symbolizing protection, honor, and spiritual strength.

Cultural Symbols and Heirlooms: Many South Asian knives are more than just tools; they are symbols of heritage, bravery, and identity. Knives are often passed down as family heirlooms, representing continuity and the preservation of cultural traditions.

Skilled Craftsmanship: South Asian knives are known for their intricate designs and high-quality materials. Artisans in the region are skilled in creating blades that are both functional and beautiful, often incorporating materials such as horn, bone, wood, and precious metals.

Gift-Giving Tradition: In many South Asian cultures, giving a knife as a gift is a symbol of respect and goodwill. Well-made knives are appreciated as meaningful gifts, often given to signify friendship, protection, or honor.

Influence on Global Knife Culture

South Asian knives like the kukri, katar, and pesh-kabz are admired worldwide for their unique designs, craftsmanship, and historical value. The kukri, in particular, is celebrated globally for its association with the Gurkhas and is popular among knife collectors and outdoor enthusiasts alike. South Asian knife-making techniques and styles have influenced global knife culture, inspiring artisans and collectors around the world.

Summary

Knife culture in South Asia reflects a balance of practicality, tradition, and artistry. Knives are integral to daily life in rural areas, martial traditions, and cultural ceremonies, symbolizing resilience, heritage, and skill. Whether used for survival, defense, or ritual, knives hold a special place in the cultural identity of South Asian countries.

East Asia

Knife culture in East Asian countries is distinguished by its combination of practicality, craftsmanship, martial tradition, and culinary importance. Each country in East Asia has its own unique knife traditions that reflect cultural values, historical influences, and artistic approaches to blade-making. Knives in East Asia are not only functional tools but also symbols of heritage and, in some cases, spirituality. Here's a look at knife culture across Mongolia, China, Japan, South Korea, and Taiwan:

Mongolia

Mongol Bichig: Mongolia's knife culture is deeply tied to its nomadic heritage and the harsh, rugged landscape that has shaped the daily lives of its people. The historical and predominant knife in Mongolia is the *mongol bichig*, also commonly known as the *Mongolian utility knife*. These knives are essential, multifunctional tools used by nomads for a variety of purposes, such as skinning animals, preparing food, and crafting. The design of the *mongol bichig* is simple yet effective, with a sturdy, straight or slightly curved blade and a handle that is often made from wood, horn, or bone. These knives reflect a utilitarian philosophy, emphasizing practicality over ornamentation. The *mongol bichig* has historically been carried by men and women alike, symbolizing the self-sufficiency and resourcefulness of the Mongolian people.

Craftsmanship: Knife craftsmanship in Mongolia is an art passed down through generations. Mongolian bladesmiths use traditional forging techniques, often crafting knives by hand to ensure their durability and sharpness. The handles are carefully shaped to provide a comfortable grip, crucial for tasks performed in Mongolia's harsh climate. While the primary focus is on function, many knives are also decorated with subtle engravings or inlays, often inspired by traditional Mongolian patterns and symbols, such as images of animals or elements of the vast Mongolian steppe. The scabbards, made from leather or wood, are sometimes adorned with ornate metal fittings, adding a touch of elegance to these otherwise rugged tools.

Regulations: Regulations surrounding knives in Mongolia are relatively lenient, reflecting their necessity in everyday life, particularly among rural and nomadic populations. Knives are considered essential for survival rather than as weapons. Consequently, they are widely accepted and commonly carried by people in rural areas. In urban centers, however, there are some restrictions on carrying knives in public spaces to ensure safety and prevent violence. Tourists and visitors are generally allowed to purchase and carry knives as souvenirs, provided they adhere to guidelines regarding transportation and display. Overall, knives in Mongolia are viewed as indispensable tools of daily life, embodying the enduring spirit of the country's nomadic culture.

China

The Dao and Jian: Traditional Chinese weapons include the *dao* (single-edged broadsword) and *jian* (double-edged straight sword). While these are larger than knives, smaller dao-like blades are common in rural areas and are used for various utility tasks. The *niuweidao* (ox-tail saber) is a traditional Chinese blade that has a curved, single-edged design and was historically used by soldiers.

Utility and Agricultural Knives: In rural China, knives are essential tools for farming, animal processing, and household tasks. Farmers and laborers commonly use heavy cleavers and dao-style knives to cut through dense vegetation, chop wood, and prepare food. Many families own a "Chinese cleaver" (chopper), which is versatile enough to handle tasks like slicing, chopping, and crushing.

Martial Arts and Wushu: Knives are integral to various forms of Chinese martial arts, such as *Wushu* and *Kung Fu*, where practitioners train with weapons for discipline, skill, and self-defense. Blades are used in martial arts demonstrations to show skill in handling and technique, with traditional weapons passed down through schools and lineages.

Artisanal and Spiritual Craftsmanship: Chinese knife-making includes intricate details, especially in decorative daggers and ceremonial knives. Knives are sometimes used as amulets or symbols in Taoist and Buddhist rituals, believed to protect the user from harm. Artisans in regions like Longquan are famous for producing high-quality, hand-forged blades with elaborate engravings and designs.

Japan

The Katana and Tantō: While not everyday knives, the *katana* (Japanese sword) and *tantō* (small dagger) are iconic in Japanese culture, symbolizing the samurai spirit, honor, and craftsmanship. The katana represents Japan's historical martial culture and is revered as an art form. The tantō was used as a samurai's sidearm and was also valued for its utility and defensive capability.

Everyday and Utility Knives: Japanese utility knives, such as the *higo no kami* (a simple, folding knife), are popular for everyday carry and general tasks. These knives are known for their minimalist design and practicality, used by craftspeople, carpenters, and artisans.

Culinary Knives: Japan is world-renowned for its high-quality kitchen knives, such as the *gyuto* (chef's knife), *santoku* (general-purpose knife), and *deba* (fish filleting knife). Japanese culinary knives are made with extreme precision, often using traditional forging techniques and high-carbon steel. Japanese chefs regard their knives as extensions of their skills, and proper knife care and technique are essential aspects of Japanese culinary training.

Cultural and Spiritual Significance: Knives in Japan carry spiritual significance, especially swords and daggers, which are believed to embody the spirit of their maker and the warrior who wields them. This connection extends to kitchen knives, with rituals like the *hocho shiki* (knife ceremony) performed at some shrines, where knives are used to prepare offerings without being touched by hand. Japanese knife-making is considered an art form, and master blacksmiths often dedicate their lives to perfecting the craft.

South Korea

The Hwachae Knives: Korean blades, such as *hwachae* (traditional chopping knives), are commonly used in food preparation, particularly for slicing vegetables and preparing *banchan* (side dishes). These knives are essential in Korean kitchens, where they are used to create the thin cuts and precise techniques needed for Korean cuisine.

Traditional Knives for Outdoor Activities: South Koreans who live in rural areas or engage in farming and outdoor activities use knives for tasks like cutting vegetation and preparing food. Utility knives similar to *jangdo* (small knives) are also carried by people who need versatile tools in outdoor or rural settings.

The Jangdo as a Personal Knife: Historically, the *jangdo* was a small, concealed knife carried by Korean men and women for self-defense and emergencies. It was considered a symbol of social status and personal protection, often decorated with traditional designs. In modern times, jangdo knives are valued as decorative or collectible items rather than functional tools.

Martial Arts and Hwa Rang Do: Some Korean martial arts, such as *Hwa Rang Do*, include knife techniques as part of training. Practitioners learn to handle blades for self-defense and to demonstrate skill in weapon-based forms, with knives representing discipline, honor, and martial skill.

Taiwan

Traditional Taiwanese Dao Knives: In Taiwan, traditional *dao*-style knives are commonly used in rural and mountainous areas, where they serve as versatile tools for clearing vegetation, hunting, and household tasks. These knives are similar in function to machetes and are integral to indigenous communities and farmers.

Paiwan Tribe and Decorative Knives: The indigenous Paiwan people of Taiwan are known for their decorative knives, which often feature intricate carvings and inlaid materials. These knives are both ceremonial and functional, used in rituals and as a symbol of tribal identity and status.

Culinary Knives and Chinese Influence: Taiwan's culinary culture includes the use of Chinese-style cleavers and other kitchen knives for preparing traditional dishes. Professional chefs and home cooks value high-quality knives, particularly for seafood and vegetable preparation, essential to Taiwanese cuisine.

Artisan Knife-Making: Taiwanese knife-makers blend traditional Chinese knife-making techniques with local designs. Artisans often create custom-made knives that are both practical and artistic, emphasizing quality and local craftsmanship.

Common Themes Across East Asian Knife Culture

Heritage and Martial Tradition: East Asian countries have long histories of martial traditions where knives and swords play important roles. In Japan and China, weapons like the katana and dao are not only functional but deeply symbolic, representing honor, discipline, and the warrior spirit. Knives also play a role in martial arts training across the region.

High-Quality Craftsmanship: East Asian knives are known for their craftsmanship, with countries like Japan and China producing some of the finest blades in the world. Artisans take great pride in using traditional forging methods to create knives with high-quality steel, intricate designs, and long-lasting durability. Many knives are passed down as family heirlooms and are seen as works of art.

Culinary Importance: In East Asia, kitchen knives are essential tools, especially in countries like Japan and China, where culinary knives are crafted to precise standards. Japanese and Chinese chefs place great emphasis on knife skills, and knife care is considered integral to cooking techniques. Each type of knife has a specific purpose, from vegetable cutting to fish filleting, reflecting the culinary diversity and skill in East Asian cuisine.

Symbolism and Spiritual Beliefs: Knives and swords carry symbolic and spiritual weight in East Asian cultures. For instance, the Japanese view blades as sacred, often associating them with purity and craftsmanship. In China, knives can have spiritual or protective qualities, with certain knives used in rituals or ceremonies to bring good fortune or ward off negative energy.

Gift and Cultural Significance: Knives are often given as gifts in East Asian countries, symbolizing respect, protection, or honor. A high-quality knife can be a meaningful gift for milestones, such as graduations or career achievements, especially among culinary professionals and artisans.

Influence on Global Knife Culture

East Asian knives, especially Japanese culinary knives and Chinese cleavers, have gained worldwide popularity. Japanese knives like the gyuto and santoku are considered some of the best in professional kitchens, known for their sharpness and precision. Similarly, Chinese cleavers have become a staple in many kitchens due to their versatility. East Asian blade-making techniques, such as the Japanese art of folding steel to create a stronger blade, have influenced knife-making traditions globally.

Summary

Knife culture in East Asia combines functionality with a profound respect for tradition, craftsmanship, and symbolism. Knives are integral to daily life, martial arts, and culinary arts, and they carry cultural significance that reflects each country's history and values. East Asian knives are admired worldwide for their quality and artistry, symbolizing the region's dedication to skill, respect, and heritage.

South East Asia

Knife culture in Southeast Asian countries is vibrant and deeply influenced by the region's history, martial traditions, and practical needs. Knives and blades serve as essential tools for daily life, symbols of cultural identity, and integral components of martial arts systems. Each country in Southeast Asia has its own unique knife traditions, reflecting a blend of indigenous practices, craftsmanship, and cultural symbolism. Here's an exploration of knife culture across countries like the Philippines, Indonesia, Malaysia, Thailand, and Myanmar:

Philippines

The Bolo and Itak: The *bolo* is one of the most iconic Filipino knives, a versatile tool with a curved, single-edged blade, commonly used in agriculture for clearing vegetation, chopping wood, and harvesting. *Itak*, a similar type of blade, is specific to the Tagalog region and used for farming, survival, and self-defense.

The Kris: The *kris* (or *kalis*) is a traditional Filipino dagger known for its wavy blade, symbolizing power and spiritual protection. It is often associated with warrior culture and is considered both a weapon and a work of art. The kris is highly valued as an heirloom and is passed down through generations, representing heritage and bravery.

Martial Arts – Eskrima/Kali/Arnis: Knives are integral to Filipino martial arts, especially *Eskrima*, *Kali*, and *Arnis*, where practitioners train with blades to develop speed, coordination, and skill in self-defense. Techniques for using and defending against knives are deeply ingrained in Filipino martial arts, which emphasize flow, reflex, and precision.

Symbolism and Craftsmanship: Filipino knives are often decorated with intricate designs, especially the kris, with ornate handles and scabbards. These knives are respected as cultural artifacts, with certain pieces treated as sacred items. Knife-makers in the Philippines are skilled artisans who create blades that are both functional and artistic.

Indonesia

The Kris (Keris): The *kris* is a sacred blade in Indonesian culture, especially in Java and Bali. Known for its distinctive wavy or straight blade and intricate handle designs, the kris is considered a symbol of spiritual power, protection, and social status. Owning a kris is seen as a sign of respect and honor, and each blade is believed to have its own mystical properties.

The Golok and Parang: The *golok* and *parang* are versatile blades used throughout Indonesia, particularly for agricultural tasks, chopping wood, and clearing jungle vegetation. Both have heavy blades suited to the tropical environment, where they are essential for rural and survival tasks.

Pencak Silat and Blade Training: In the Indonesian martial art of *Pencak Silat*, knives play a significant role. Practitioners learn techniques for both offense and defense, training with blades such as the kris, golok, and small daggers like the *badik*. Silat emphasizes fluid movements, deception, and adaptability, with knife techniques that reflect these principles.

Ritual and Symbolic Value: The kris is often used in ceremonies and rituals, including blessings, weddings, and other important events. In some families, krises are believed to contain spirits or energies and are kept as heirlooms, with rituals performed to honor them. Many krises feature elaborate engravings and inlays, reflecting Indonesia's artistic heritage.

Malaysia

The Parang: The *parang* is a traditional Malaysian machete used for agricultural work and jungle survival. With a sturdy blade that can cut through thick vegetation, the parang is indispensable in rural areas and is also widely used by indigenous communities for daily tasks and hunting.

The Kris (Keris): Similar to Indonesia, the kris holds deep cultural and spiritual significance in Malaysia, particularly among Malay people. The kris is seen as a symbol of bravery and status, and it is often worn by men during formal ceremonies, weddings, and cultural events as a sign of heritage and pride.

Silat and Blade Work: The Malaysian martial art *Silat* incorporates various knife techniques, using weapons like the kris, parang, and *pisau* (small knife). Silat practitioners are trained to use knives in close combat, with an emphasis on fluid, evasive movements and quick strikes.

Artisan Craftsmanship: Malay krises and parangs are often hand-crafted, with handles and scabbards featuring intricate carvings and inlaid materials. The craftsmanship reflects local symbols and patterns, making each blade unique and culturally significant. These knives are treasured as family heirlooms and are sometimes passed down for generations.

Thailand

The E-toh (Cleaver): In Thai culture, the *e-toh*, a heavy-duty cleaver, is used for various tasks, especially in rural areas. It is versatile enough for chopping wood, cutting meat, and even preparing traditional dishes. The e-toh is a common tool in rural kitchens and is highly valued for its durability and functionality.

The Daab: The *daab* is a traditional Thai sword used in martial arts, especially *Krabi-Krabong*, the weapon-based martial art of Thailand. Though it is a larger weapon, its single-edged design shares similarities with knife techniques and has influenced the way knives are used in Thai combat styles.

Muay Thai and Knife Self-Defense: While *Muay Thai* is primarily an unarmed martial art, traditional Thai martial arts like *Muay Boran* and Krabi-Krabong include knife techniques for self-defense. Practitioners learn methods to control and counter knife attacks, with an emphasis on body movement and evasion.

Utility and Rural Knives: In rural Thailand, knives are essential tools for farming, fishing, and cooking. Traditional knives are designed for versatility, with thick blades suited to the tropical environment. Knife-making is a respected skill, and Thai knives often feature sturdy construction to withstand heavy use.

Myanmar (Burma)

The Dha: The *dha* is a traditional Burmese blade with a single-edged, slightly curved design, used for utility and self-defense. Often resembling a short sword or long knife, the dha is used by farmers, hunters, and craftsmen in rural Myanmar for cutting, carving, and chopping tasks.

Martial Arts – Bando: In the Burmese martial art *Bando*, practitioners train with blades such as the dha, using techniques that emphasize fluidity, speed, and control.

Bando teaches both offensive and defensive knife skills, drawing from the traditional warrior culture of Myanmar.

Ceremonial Use and Artisan Craftsmanship: High-quality dha swords and knives are decorated with elaborate carvings and metalwork, particularly on the handles and scabbards. These knives are valued as cultural artifacts and are often displayed during religious and cultural ceremonies as symbols of strength and heritage.

Everyday Use and Rural Life: In Myanmar's rural communities, knives are essential for daily tasks, from farming and building to cooking and animal processing. Artisans craft durable, practical knives that are designed to handle rugged conditions and heavy-duty work.

Cambodia

The Daab and Cleaver: Cambodians use large knives similar to cleavers for agricultural work, as well as the *daab* (a single-edged sword used in traditional Cambodian martial arts). These knives are used for cutting, chopping, and other labor-intensive tasks in rural areas.

Martial Arts and Pradal Serey: Traditional Cambodian martial arts, including *Pradal Serey* and *Kbach Kun Boran*, sometimes incorporate weapons training, including knife techniques. Practitioners learn both offensive and defensive knife handling skills, which are valued as part of Cambodia's warrior heritage.

Cultural and Artistic Knives: Cambodian knives are often decorated with traditional symbols and patterns, especially those crafted by artisans in regions like Phnom Penh. While some knives are purely utilitarian, others serve as decorative items in homes, symbolizing strength and self-reliance.

Common Themes Across Southeast Asian Knife Culture

Practical Utility and Rural Life: In rural areas across Southeast Asia, knives are essential tools used for farming, hunting, fishing, and general household tasks. Blades like the parang, bolo, and golok are designed for heavy-duty work in tropical environments, where they are indispensable for everyday survival.

Martial Arts and Warrior Heritage: Knives hold a prominent place in Southeast Asian martial arts, such as Silat in Indonesia and Malaysia, Kali in the Philippines, and Bando in Myanmar. These arts emphasize knife techniques for self-defense, control, and adaptability, preserving the region's warrior culture and blade skills.

Ceremonial and Spiritual Significance: Many knives, especially the kris in Indonesia and Malaysia, carry spiritual and ceremonial value. They are believed to have protective qualities or supernatural powers, and are often kept as family heirlooms, blessed in rituals, or displayed in ceremonies to represent heritage and strength.

Artisan Craftsmanship: Knives in Southeast Asia are often decorated with intricate carvings and inlays, showcasing the skill of local artisans. The designs reflect regional symbols and styles, with handles and scabbards crafted from wood, horn, bone, and metals. These knives are appreciated both as functional tools and as pieces of art.

Influence on Global Knife Culture

Southeast Asian knives like the kris, kukri, and parang have had a significant impact on global knife culture, admired for their unique designs, historical importance, and martial applications. Filipino martial arts, particularly Kali and

Eskrima, have gained international popularity, with knife techniques that are taught worldwide for self-defense. The practical, durable designs of blades like the parang and bolo have also influenced modern survival and bushcraft knives, used by outdoor enthusiasts globally.

Summary

Knife culture in Southeast Asia combines practicality with deep cultural significance. Knives are essential tools in everyday life, symbols of heritage and spiritual power, and respected weapons within martial traditions. The region's rich history, craftsmanship, and diverse knife designs continue to be celebrated both locally and internationally, reflecting the unique cultural fabric of Southeast Asia.

North Africa

Knife culture in North African countries is shaped by the region's rich history, diverse ethnic groups, and unique blend of Arab, Berber, and African influences. Knives hold a special place in North African culture as practical tools, symbols of identity, objects of artistry, and essential components of martial traditions. From the ornate daggers of Morocco to the utilitarian blades of Egypt and Sudan, knives in North Africa reflect both function and cultural pride. Here's an exploration of knife culture across countries like Morocco, Algeria, Tunisia, Egypt, and Sudan:

Morocco

The Koummya: The *koummya* is a traditional Moroccan dagger known for its curved blade and elaborate, decorated hilt and scabbard. Originating among the Berber people, the koummya is symbolic of Moroccan heritage and is often carried during ceremonies or as part of traditional attire, especially in the Atlas Mountains and Berber regions.

Symbolism and Social Status: The koummya is more than a weapon—it's a symbol of social status and regional identity. Owning a finely crafted koummya signifies respect and tradition, and the dagger is often passed down through generations as a family heirloom.

Craftsmanship and Artistic Detail: Moroccan artisans craft koummya knives with intricate silver or brass inlays, engravings, and geometric patterns. The handles are often made from wood, horn, or bone, and some of the more elaborate koummyas feature jewel inlays. This decorative style showcases Morocco's rich tradition of metalwork and artistic detail.

Utility and Practical Use: In rural Morocco, knives are still essential tools for daily tasks such as farming, food preparation, and animal care. Small knives and utility blades are commonly used by farmers and herders, reflecting a practical side to Moroccan knife culture.

Algeria

The Flyssa: The *flyssa* is a traditional Algerian blade with a narrow, single-edged design, often carried by the Kabyle people of the Atlas Mountains. It features a distinctive triangular blade and is decorated with intricate designs, representing Kabyle identity and craftsmanship.

Berber Culture and Symbolism: The flyssa is more than a practical tool; it embodies Berber heritage and is often decorated with Berber symbols, including geometric and floral patterns. Flyssas are prized as family heirlooms, signifying honor, courage, and tribal pride.

Craftsmanship and Artistry: Algerian knife-makers create flyssa blades using traditional techniques, often adding engraved patterns and intricate handle designs. The handles are usually made from wood or horn and may be inlaid with metals, showcasing local artistry.

Practical Use in Rural Areas: In rural Algerian communities, knives are used for farming, hunting, and daily chores. Many people carry small utility knives for practical purposes, particularly in Berber villages where traditional skills and crafts are still widely valued.

Tunisia

The Jambiya: Similar to other parts of North Africa and the Middle East, the *jambiya* (curved dagger) holds cultural significance in Tunisia. Though its use has declined over time, it remains an important symbol of Tunisian heritage, especially among Bedouin and Berber communities.

Symbolic and Decorative Knives: Tunisian knives are often crafted with a focus on decoration, incorporating elements of Islamic and Berber art. Knives used in ceremonial contexts are frequently adorned with designs inspired by local cultural and religious symbols.

Utility and Traditional Knives: In rural Tunisia, knives are essential tools for agricultural work, including harvesting and animal processing. Utility knives are commonly used by farmers and herders and are often simple in design but highly valued for their durability and practicality.

Craftsmanship and Market Traditions: Tunisian souks (markets) often feature handmade knives, crafted by local artisans who continue the tradition of metalworking. These knives, including decorative jambiyas and utility blades, reflect Tunisia's rich history of craftsmanship and are often sold as collector's items or souvenirs.

Egypt

The Khanjar and Shafra: The *khanjar* (curved dagger) is traditionally associated with Arab and Bedouin cultures and is sometimes worn for ceremonial purposes in Egypt, particularly in Sinai. The *shafra* is a smaller knife commonly carried by Egyptian farmers and workers for practical tasks.

Historical Influence and Weaponry: Ancient Egypt had a rich history of using knives and daggers, both for utility and as symbols of power. Knives made from bronze and later iron were used for everything from daily tasks to religious ceremonies. In modern Egypt, knives are more commonly practical tools, especially in rural communities where they are essential for agricultural work.

Utility Knives in Daily Life: In Egypt's rural areas, knives are necessary for farming, animal care, and food preparation. Many Egyptians carry small utility knives for daily tasks, particularly in regions like Upper Egypt, where traditional practices are still observed.

Craftsmanship and Market Knives: Egyptian markets sell a variety of knives, often handmade by local artisans. These knives are generally simple but functional, with wooden or metal handles, and are designed to be practical tools for farmers, fishermen, and craftsmen.

Sudan

The Mandingo Knife: The *Mandingo knife*, named after the Mandingo people, is commonly used in Sudan and has a simple design with a straight blade and an ornate handle. It is primarily used for hunting, protection, and ceremonial purposes among tribes in Sudan and neighboring areas.

Traditional Tribal Knives: In Sudan's tribal communities, knives are essential for daily tasks such as hunting, animal processing, and food preparation. These knives are often decorated with tribal patterns and symbols that signify cultural identity and clan affiliation.

The Role of Knives in Everyday Life: In rural Sudan, knives are practical tools for pastoralists and farmers, used for tending livestock, preparing food, and performing basic repairs. Many people in rural areas carry utility knives, which are often simple in design but valued for their versatility and durability.

Craftsmanship and Cultural Value: Sudanese knives are frequently handmade by local artisans, with attention to the cultural details of each tribe or region. The knives may feature leather sheaths or engraved handles and are sometimes passed down through families as valuable items of cultural heritage.

Common Themes Across North African Knife Culture

Symbolism and Social Identity: Knives in North Africa are often symbolic of social status, regional identity, and cultural pride. Items like the Moroccan koummya, Algerian flyssa, and Tunisian jambiya are more than functional tools; they are symbols of heritage, tradition, and honor, often passed down as family heirlooms or given as prestigious gifts.

Artisan Craftsmanship: North African knives are known for their intricate designs, with handles and scabbards adorned with patterns that reflect local traditions. Metalwork, engravings, and inlaid materials are common, showcasing the region's highly developed artisan skills. Many knives are crafted by hand in markets or workshops, making each piece unique and culturally significant.

Practical Utility in Rural Life: Across North Africa, knives are indispensable tools in rural and agricultural communities. They are used for farming, hunting, fishing, and everyday chores, serving as essential tools for self-sufficiency. Many North Africans carry small knives for daily tasks, reflecting the importance of practical, durable blades.

Ceremonial and Ritual Use: In addition to everyday use, knives hold ceremonial value in North African cultures. They are used in weddings, religious festivals, and traditional rites of passage. Some knives are believed to have protective qualities, particularly in Berber and Bedouin communities, where they are viewed as symbols of spiritual strength and personal protection.

Martial and Historical Influence: North Africa's history of warfare and tribal conflicts has influenced its knife culture, with certain blades originating as weapons. Although most traditional knives are now primarily ceremonial, they retain the aesthetic and symbolic elements of their martial past, representing courage and resilience.

Influence on Global Knife Culture

North African knives, particularly the koummya, flyssa, and jambiya, are admired worldwide for their unique designs and intricate craftsmanship. Collectors and historians appreciate these blades for their cultural heritage, and many artisans outside North Africa have drawn inspiration from North African patterns, shapes, and metalwork techniques. In addition, the versatility and durability of North African utility knives have made them popular among outdoor and survival enthusiasts.

Summary

Knife culture in North Africa is a rich blend of practicality, artistry, and cultural symbolism. Knives are indispensable in daily life, especially in rural areas, where they are tools of survival and self-sufficiency. At the same time, ceremonial and decorative knives carry a deep sense of heritage and identity, reflecting the craftsmanship and values of North African communities. Whether as practical tools or symbols of heritage, knives are deeply ingrained in North African culture and continue to be celebrated for their historical and cultural significance.

Central Africa

Knife culture in Central African countries is deeply rooted in the region's history, indigenous traditions, and practical needs. Knives and blades serve as essential tools for daily life in rural areas and are valued for their ceremonial and symbolic roles. In places like the Democratic Republic of the Congo, Central African Republic, Cameroon, Chad, and Gabon, knives also hold historical significance, often symbolizing social status, spirituality, and cultural identity. Here's a look at knife culture across Central African countries:

Democratic Republic of the Congo (DRC)

The Ikakalaka and Ngulu: The *ikakalaka* is a traditional, double-edged sword used by the Mongo and other ethnic groups in the DRC. The *ngulu*, sometimes called a "execution sword," has a curved, cleaver-like blade and is associated with the tribes in the central and northern parts of the country. These ceremonial blades are often elaborately decorated, symbolizing power and tribal authority.

Symbolism and Spirituality: Knives in the DRC often carry symbolic and spiritual significance. The ngulu, for example, is considered a symbol of protection and social status and was historically used in initiation ceremonies or rituals. It is now primarily used as a ceremonial item, embodying power and spiritual beliefs.

Craftsmanship and Artistry: Congolese artisans craft knives with distinctive shapes and intricate designs. Many ceremonial knives feature engravings, patterns, and materials like ivory or brass. The level of craftsmanship reflects the importance of these knives in traditional Congolese society.

Utility and Daily Life: In rural areas, knives are indispensable tools for hunting, agriculture, and food preparation. Machetes and small utility knives are commonly used for clearing land, gathering food, and performing household tasks.

Central African Republic (CAR)

The Throwing Knife (Hunga Munga): The *hunga munga* is a traditional, multi-bladed throwing knife used by various tribes in Central Africa, including the Zande and Ngbaka peoples. These knives have distinct, wing-like blades and were traditionally used in combat and hunting, though they are now largely ceremonial.

Ceremonial and Symbolic Use: The hunga munga is often displayed as a symbol of status and cultural heritage. In many communities, these knives are passed down through generations and serve as valuable family heirlooms. They are also used in certain initiation and coming-of-age ceremonies, symbolizing courage and skill.

Practical Knives in Rural Life: In rural parts of the CAR, knives and machetes are vital tools for daily survival. Farmers and hunters rely on them for clearing brush, farming, and hunting, while households use knives for cooking and preparation. These utilitarian blades are straightforward in design and crafted for functionality.

Craftsmanship and Indigenous Techniques: Central African artisans often create knives using traditional metalworking techniques, and the handles may be decorated with tribal patterns or symbols. The distinctive shapes and styles of knives reflect the region's diverse ethnic and cultural backgrounds.

Cameroon

The Mbola and Fang Knife: The *mbola* is a knife used by the Tikar and other ethnic groups in Cameroon. It has a short, broad blade and is often used for agricultural tasks. In addition, the Fang people of Cameroon use a traditional knife with a single-edged blade and distinctive handle designs that represent cultural identity.

Spiritual and Ceremonial Knives: In Cameroon, knives are sometimes used in traditional rituals, representing spiritual protection or warrior identity. Some tribal knives are considered sacred and are used in ceremonies, particularly among the Fang and other forest-dwelling communities.

Practical Use in Farming and Hunting: In rural Cameroon, knives are essential tools for agriculture, hunting, and food preparation. Farmers use these knives for tasks like harvesting crops, preparing food, and clearing land. Many Cameroonians also carry small utility knives for practical tasks.

Artisan Knife-Making: Cameroonian knives are crafted with handles made from wood or animal bone, often decorated with tribal symbols and patterns. Blacksmiths and artisans in Cameroon are skilled at making durable, practical knives that also reflect local artistry and cultural pride.

Chad

The Gile Knife: The *gile* knife is a small utility knife commonly used by the people of Chad, especially by nomadic groups like the Toubou and the Fulani. It is used for various daily tasks, including hunting, animal care, and food preparation.

Ceremonial Knives and Status Symbols: In some Chadian communities, decorated knives are worn as part of traditional attire, symbolizing social status, strength, or warrior identity. These ceremonial knives are often engraved with local patterns, reflecting the wearer's clan or tribe.

Survival and Utility in Nomadic Life: For nomadic groups in Chad, knives are essential survival tools used for tasks such as animal husbandry, shelter building, and food preparation. Many nomads carry a knife as part of their daily essentials, relying on it for a variety of purposes in the challenging desert environment.

Craftsmanship and Cultural Significance: Knives in Chad are often crafted by local blacksmiths, who shape blades to meet the practical needs of the community. Handles may be made from wood, bone, or horn, and decorated with simple carvings or tribal markings that reflect the local culture.

Gabon

The Fang Machete: In Gabon, the Fang ethnic group traditionally uses a machete with a broad, heavy blade, essential for clearing vegetation in the rainforests. These machetes are multipurpose tools used for agricultural tasks, construction, and hunting.

Ceremonial Knives and Tribal Identity: In Gabon, certain tribes use knives in ceremonial contexts, symbolizing protection and strength. Knives are sometimes used in traditional dances or rituals to represent bravery or spiritual guidance. Decorative knives can serve as symbols of tribal identity, particularly among the Fang and other forest communities.

Hunting and Practical Use: For Gabon's indigenous communities, knives are critical for hunting, fishing, and building shelter. Hunters and gatherers rely on machetes and small knives to navigate the dense forests, making them essential for survival.

Artisanal Craftsmanship and Symbolism: Gabonese knives, especially those used by the Fang, are often decorated with traditional patterns or symbolic engravings. Local blacksmiths craft these blades with attention to both durability and aesthetic, making them both functional and culturally significant.

Common Themes Across Central African Knife Culture

Practical Use and Survival: Knives and machetes are crucial tools in Central Africa, especially in rural and forested areas where they are used for farming, hunting, and daily survival tasks. In places where agriculture and subsistence hunting are common, knives are indispensable for gathering food, clearing land, and building shelter.

Ceremonial and Cultural Symbolism: Many Central African knives hold ceremonial or symbolic significance, used in rites of passage, religious rituals, or traditional dances. Knives like the ngulu and hunga munga are often kept as symbols of clan identity and ancestral heritage, representing strength, protection, and spiritual beliefs.

Artisan Craftsmanship and Tribal Design: Central African knives are often decorated with engravings, carvings, and inlays that reflect tribal patterns or cultural symbols. Skilled artisans create knives that serve as both tools and works of art, showcasing the region's rich tradition of metalwork and craftsmanship.

Social Status and Clan Identity: In many Central African communities, a person's knife or blade can signify social status, clan affiliation, or family heritage. Decorative knives are passed down through generations, symbolizing respect and pride, and are sometimes worn as part of traditional dress during important events.

Martial and Defensive Roles: Historically, certain knives and throwing blades were used for self-defense and warfare among tribes in Central Africa. Although they are now largely ceremonial, these knives retain their martial symbolism, representing bravery and warrior traditions in the region.

Influence on Global Knife Culture

Central African knives, especially unique designs like the hunga munga and ngulu, are admired by collectors and historians for their cultural heritage and distinctive shapes. The throwing knife tradition, as seen in the hunga munga, has influenced weapon collectors and martial artists worldwide, who study these designs for their ingenuity and historical importance. Additionally, the robust, practical nature of Central African machetes and utility knives has influenced the design of survival knives used in rugged environments globally.

Summary

Knife culture in Central Africa reflects a blend of practicality, artistry, and cultural symbolism. Knives are indispensable for daily tasks in rural areas, embodying self-sufficiency and survival, while ceremonial knives reflect social status, spiritual beliefs, and heritage. Through their distinct designs and cultural significance, Central African knives continue to represent the strength, resilience, and artistic heritage of the region's diverse communities.

Western Africa

Knife culture in West African countries is vibrant and multifaceted, shaped by the region's diverse ethnic groups, historical significance of traditional weapons, and practical needs in everyday life. Knives in countries like Nigeria, Ghana, Mali, Senegal, and Burkina Faso are essential for both utility and cultural expression. They are tools for farming, hunting, and household use and also serve ceremonial, symbolic, and martial roles. Here's a deeper look into the knife culture across West African countries:

Nigeria

The Ada and Idoma Dagger: Among the Igbo people, the *ada* is a ceremonial machete, while the *idoma dagger* is significant in Idoma culture. Both are used in traditional ceremonies, with the ada symbolizing authority and warrior status in the Igbo culture. The ada is usually decorated and carried by chiefs or during festivals.

Traditional and Ceremonial Use: Nigerian knives and short swords are often used in ceremonial contexts, where they represent social status, tribal identity, and authority. The ada, for example, is a symbol of leadership among the Igbo, and it is presented during rites of passage and other cultural events.

Practical Use in Agriculture and Hunting: Machetes and knives are indispensable in Nigeria's agricultural communities, used for clearing fields, harvesting crops, and processing food. Hunters also rely on knives for bushmeat hunting, and utility knives are common household tools.

Craftsmanship and Artistry: In Nigeria, artisans make decorative knives with carved handles and patterned blades, often using local materials like wood, brass, and leather. These knives showcase Nigerian craftsmanship, with designs that reflect tribal symbols and historical motifs.

Ghana

The Akrafena: The *akrafena* is a traditional Ashanti sword, symbolizing power, bravery, and spiritual protection. Although it is a sword, the akrafena is used similarly to ceremonial knives in other cultures, primarily as a symbol of authority and pride. It features a broad blade with an elaborate hilt, often carried during ceremonies.

Utility Knives and Agricultural Tools: In Ghana's rural communities, knives and machetes are used daily in farming, hunting, and cooking. Farmers use machetes to clear land, harvest crops like cocoa and yams, and prepare food. These tools are essential to life in agricultural settings.

Symbolism and Spirituality: The akrafena holds spiritual value in Ashanti culture, believed to protect the soul and honor ancestors. This sword is used in rituals, carried by chiefs, and sometimes placed in shrines as a symbol of ancestral protection.

Craftsmanship and Pride: Ghanaian blacksmiths create knives and machetes with attention to detail, often adding carved wooden handles and etched patterns on the blades. These blades are both functional and ornamental, reflecting local artistry and pride in craftsmanship.

Mali

The Tellem and Fulani Knives: The *tellem* knife, traditionally used by the Dogon people, is a small, versatile blade used for agricultural and daily tasks. The *fulani knife*, commonly used by the nomadic Fulani people, is a simple, practical tool designed for animal care and survival.

Symbolic Use Among the Dogon and Fulani: Among the Dogon people, knives are symbolic in ritual ceremonies, particularly in initiation rites. The Fulani, known for their nomadic lifestyle, carry knives as essential survival tools, representing self-reliance and adaptability in the Sahel.

Ceremonial Significance: The Dogon use knives in traditional religious practices and dances, where they symbolize protection and spiritual strength. These knives are often decorated and handled with care, embodying a connection to the Dogon's complex belief system and cosmology.

Craftsmanship and Community Skills: In Mali, knives are often handcrafted by blacksmiths who are respected in the community for their skill. These artisans craft knives that are not only functional but also reflect cultural aesthetics, using materials like leather, bone, and wood for handles and scabbards.

Senegal

The Ndiang Knife: The *ndiang* is a traditional Senegalese knife used by the Wolof and Serer people for agricultural tasks, hunting, and food preparation. This knife is simple yet effective, and it has a straight, sturdy blade designed for durability.

Hunting and Agricultural Use: In rural Senegal, knives and machetes are essential tools for farming and hunting. Hunters use them to process bushmeat, while farmers rely on them to clear fields, harvest crops, and perform other tasks.

Ceremonial Knives and Traditional Authority: Among Senegal's various ethnic groups, knives sometimes serve as symbols of authority and are used in ceremonial contexts. Some leaders and healers may carry decorated knives as signs of their status and role within the community.

Artisanal Craftsmanship and Design: Senegalese artisans craft knives with practical designs, often adding patterns or carvings to the handles and sheaths. The artistry reflects local traditions and makes the knives both functional and culturally meaningful.

Burkina Faso

The Lobi Knife and Mossi Swords: Among the Lobi people, knives and short swords are both functional tools and symbols of defense. The *lobi knife* is a simple, rugged blade used for farming and hunting, while the *mossi swords* of the Mossi ethnic group are more ceremonial, representing warrior identity and leadership.

Spiritual and Cultural Significance: In certain Burkinabé communities, knives and blades are used in rituals and initiation ceremonies, symbolizing courage and maturity. For example, Mossi swords are carried by community leaders or warriors during festivals as signs of protection and honor.

Utility Knives in Farming and Daily Life: For the people of Burkina Faso, knives are critical for farming and everyday tasks. Machetes and smaller utility knives are commonly used to cut crops, prepare food, and manage livestock, highlighting the region's agricultural lifestyle.

Decorative and Functional Craftsmanship: Burkinabé artisans create knives with simple, sturdy designs, often adding carved handles or leather sheaths. The materials used are locally sourced, and the blades are designed to withstand heavy use, reflecting both functionality and traditional aesthetics.

Common Themes Across West African Knife Culture

Practical Utility in Agriculture and Hunting: In rural West Africa, knives and machetes are essential tools for farming, hunting, and household chores. They are used for clearing land, harvesting crops, cutting meat, and preparing food, making them indispensable to daily life in agricultural communities.

Ceremonial and Symbolic Use: Knives hold ceremonial significance in many West African cultures. They are often used in rituals, festivals, and traditional rites of passage, symbolizing authority, courage, and spiritual protection. Certain knives are carried by leaders, chiefs, or spiritual figures to signify their role in society.

Martial and Warrior Heritage: Blades like the ada in Nigeria and the akrafena in Ghana are rooted in warrior culture, representing bravery, honor, and strength. Although they are now primarily ceremonial, they retain their symbolic martial value and are carried during cultural events as signs of power and protection.

Artisan Craftsmanship and Cultural Pride: West African knives are often decorated with intricate designs, using locally sourced materials like wood, bone, and leather. Artisans create knives that blend functionality with beauty, adding carvings and patterns that reflect tribal identity and cultural heritage.

Social Status and Clan Identity: In many West African cultures, a person's knife can signify social status or clan affiliation. Decorative knives are often passed down through generations, symbolizing family heritage, pride, and respect. Owning a well-crafted knife is seen as a mark of dignity and respect.

Influence on Global Knife Culture

West African knives, particularly ceremonial blades like the akrafena and ada, are admired by collectors and historians worldwide for their craftsmanship, cultural heritage, and distinctive designs. The robust, practical design of West African machetes and utility knives has also inspired outdoor and survival knives globally. West African artisanship, especially in metalworking and carving, has influenced knife-making techniques and decorative styles, reflecting the region's unique contributions to global knife culture.

Summary

Knife culture in West Africa is a rich tapestry of practicality, artistry, and tradition. Knives serve essential roles in daily life, especially in agriculture and hunting, while also carrying deep cultural meaning. Through their diverse designs and functions, knives in West Africa continue to embody the strength, heritage, and identity of the region's varied communities.

East Africa

Knife culture in East African countries is shaped by the region's rich history, diverse tribal customs, and the practical needs of agricultural and pastoral lifestyles. Knives in countries like Kenya, Tanzania, Ethiopia, Uganda, and Somalia serve as essential tools for everyday life and carry significant cultural, symbolic, and ceremonial importance. Many knives reflect the unique artistic styles and martial traditions of East Africa's various ethnic groups, while others are practical tools vital to rural and nomadic communities. Here's an overview of knife culture across East African countries:

Kenya

The Panga Machete: The *panga* is one of the most iconic and commonly used knives in Kenya. With a broad, curved blade, it is an essential tool for agricultural work, clearing land, cutting wood, and food preparation. The panga is widely used across East Africa, but in Kenya, it's particularly popular among farmers and rural communities.

The Seme Knife: The *seme* is a traditional Maasai short sword with a straight or slightly curved blade, used historically by Maasai warriors. The seme symbolizes strength and bravery and is often part of Maasai warriors' traditional attire. Though now largely ceremonial, it remains a cultural symbol of Maasai heritage and identity.

Everyday Utility Knives: Smaller knives are commonly used in Kenya for a range of tasks, including herding, hunting, and household chores. These knives are valued for their practicality and durability, and they are often carried by men and women in rural communities.

Craftsmanship and Artistry: Kenyan knives, especially the seme, are often decorated with carvings or inlaid with beads on the handle, reflecting Maasai or other tribal patterns. Blacksmiths in rural areas make high-quality blades that are both functional and aesthetically pleasing, highlighting Kenya's metalworking traditions.

Tanzania

The Simi and Machetes: The *simi*, similar to the Maasai seme, is a traditional Tanzanian knife used by the Maasai and other ethnic groups. Like the seme, the simi is a short sword associated with warrior culture and is primarily ceremonial today, worn as a symbol of courage and heritage.

Knives in Pastoral Life: Among the Maasai and other pastoral communities, knives are indispensable tools used for herding, skinning animals, and gathering resources. They are part of daily life, reflecting the self-sufficient lifestyle of East African pastoralists who rely on knives for a wide range of tasks.

Hunting and Utility Knives: In rural Tanzania, knives are essential for hunting, fishing, and agricultural work. Farmers use machetes to clear land, gather firewood, and prepare food. Hunters use smaller, sharper knives for skinning and processing game, which is common in Tanzania's wildlife-rich areas.

Artisan Craftsmanship: Tanzanian knives are typically crafted with simple yet durable designs. Some knives feature beaded handles or decorative scabbards, often with designs inspired by the ethnic group of the artisan. The use of natural materials like wood, bone, and leather is common in Tanzanian knife-making.

Ethiopia

The Shotel: The *shotel* is a traditional Ethiopian curved sword with a distinctive sickle-like blade. Historically used by Ethiopian warriors, particularly the Amhara, the shotel is both a weapon and a symbol of Ethiopian heritage. Though not a knife in the strictest sense, it holds cultural value and represents Ethiopia's unique martial history.

Gurade and Small Utility Knives: The *gurade* is a traditional Ethiopian knife with a straight blade used for various practical tasks, including hunting, farming, and food preparation. Smaller utility knives are also common, used for daily tasks such as cutting, skinning, and carving.

Symbolism and Ceremonial Value: In Ethiopia, certain knives and swords are symbols of warrior status and cultural pride, especially the shotel and other historical weapons. These blades are often displayed in homes or carried during ceremonial occasions, symbolizing honor, bravery, and Ethiopian heritage.

Craftsmanship and Metalworking Tradition: Ethiopian knives and blades are often crafted by local artisans who pass down traditional metalworking techniques. Some knives feature decorated hilts and scabbards, with handles made from wood, horn, or brass, reflecting Ethiopia's dedication to artistry and craftsmanship.

Uganda

The Pangolin Knife: Named after the pangolin, this is a utility knife commonly used in Uganda for a variety of tasks. Known for its durable blade and versatility, it is especially popular in rural areas where it's used for farming, food preparation, and general household tasks.

Knives in Agricultural Communities: In Uganda, knives and machetes are indispensable in agricultural communities. Farmers use them for clearing fields, harvesting crops like bananas and coffee, and processing food. Knives are also used by fishermen on Lake Victoria for preparing their catch.

Ceremonial and Symbolic Use: Certain Ugandan tribes incorporate knives into traditional ceremonies, where they may represent strength, protection, or leadership. Decorative knives are sometimes passed down as family heirlooms, symbolizing continuity and respect for heritage.

Handcrafted and Locally Made: Ugandan knives are often handmade by local artisans who use simple designs and materials like wood and iron. These knives are crafted to be practical and long-lasting, reflecting the resourcefulness of Ugandan communities.

Somalia

The Billao: The *billao* is a traditional Somali dagger with a double-edged, leaf-shaped blade and a distinctive three-pronged hilt. Historically carried by Somali warriors, the billao is a symbol of strength, bravery, and cultural pride. Though it is now mostly ceremonial, the billao remains a key symbol of Somali identity.

Everyday and Utility Knives: In Somalia, knives are essential tools for nomadic and pastoral communities, used in herding, animal processing, and general daily tasks. Knives are also used for self-defense, reflecting the challenging environment of nomadic life in Somalia.

Symbolism and Social Status: The billao is worn by Somali men during cultural celebrations and significant life events. It is sometimes given as a gift to mark important milestones, such as coming of age or marriage, symbolizing maturity, protection, and responsibility.

Craftsmanship and Decoration: Somali knives, particularly the billao, are decorated with engravings and carvings on the handle, which may be made from materials like wood, horn, or bone. The intricate designs highlight Somali craftsmanship and the knife's role as a cultural artifact.

Common Themes Across East African Knife Culture

Essential Tools for Daily Life: In East Africa, knives are indispensable for agricultural and pastoral work, hunting, fishing, and food preparation. In rural and nomadic communities, they are critical for managing livestock, gathering resources, and maintaining self-sufficiency.

Martial Heritage and Warrior Symbolism: Knives and short swords hold significant value as symbols of warrior identity and heritage, especially among groups like the Maasai, Somali, and Ethiopian Amhara. Knives like the seme and billao represent bravery, protection, and cultural pride, and they are worn in ceremonies as expressions of traditional warrior status.

Ceremonial and Symbolic Significance: Many East African knives carry ceremonial importance, used in rituals, rites of passage, and cultural events. They symbolize social status, personal maturity, and community respect, with some knives, such as the shotel and billao, passed down as family heirlooms or given as gifts to mark life milestones.

Artisan Craftsmanship and Tribal Design: East African knives often feature traditional designs, with handles and sheaths decorated to reflect tribal patterns and heritage.

Local artisans take pride in using materials like wood, bone, and leather to create blades that are both functional and meaningful cultural items.

Social Status and Identity: In several East African cultures, a person's knife or blade can represent social rank or tribal identity. Decorative knives are highly regarded as heirlooms, embodying family honor and ancestral pride. Carrying a distinctive knife, like the billao or seme, is a way to display cultural affiliation and personal status.

Influence on Global Knife Culture

East African knives, particularly the panga machete, seme, and billao, have had an impact on global knife culture. The robust design of the panga, known for its ability to handle dense vegetation, has influenced machetes worldwide, especially among outdoor and bushcraft enthusiasts. The billao and shotel are admired by collectors for their unique designs, historical significance, and connection to East African martial traditions. Additionally, East African artisanship, with its focus on durability and tribal aesthetics, has inspired knife-making techniques and styles globally.

Summary

Knife culture in East Africa combines practicality, artistry, and deep cultural symbolism. Knives are essential tools in everyday rural life and carry significant meaning in ceremonial and cultural contexts. Through their functional designs and symbolic importance, knives in East Africa reflect the region's resilience, heritage, and connection to traditional values, continuing to hold a place of pride and utility across diverse East African communities.

Southern Africa

Knife culture in Southern African countries is deeply rooted in the region's history, indigenous traditions, and the practical needs of daily life, especially in rural and tribal communities. In countries like South Africa, Namibia, Botswana, Zimbabwe, Mozambique, and Zambia, knives are essential tools for agriculture, hunting, and self-sufficiency. Many knives also carry ceremonial and symbolic significance, serving as cultural artifacts that reflect the heritage and artistry of local communities. Here's an overview of knife culture across Southern African countries:

South Africa

The Okapi Knife: The *Okapi* is a folding knife traditionally associated with South Africa, particularly within the Xhosa and Zulu communities. Known for its durability and affordability, the Okapi knife has a distinctive clip-point blade and wooden handle. It is widely used for agricultural tasks, everyday work, and even self-defense.

The Knobkerrie and Assegai: Although not knives, the *knobkerrie* (a short club with a rounded head) and *assegai* (a traditional spear) are significant in South African culture. They represent Zulu warrior heritage and are sometimes carried during ceremonies or traditional dances.

Practical and Utility Knives: In rural South Africa, knives and machetes are essential tools for farming, cutting wood, and hunting. Many people in agricultural communities rely on knives for various tasks, and they are often kept within the household as everyday tools.

Knife-Making and Artistry: South Africa has a vibrant knife-making culture, with local artisans producing high-quality hunting and utility knives. Many artisans combine traditional designs with modern materials, creating knives that are both functional and aesthetically appealing. South African knife makers, such as Chris Reeve, have gained international recognition for their craftsmanship.

Namibia

The Herero Knife and Traditional Blades: Among the Herero people in Namibia, knives are essential tools for daily life, used in agriculture, hunting, and food preparation. The Herero often carry simple, sturdy knives that are effective for practical tasks and survival in rural settings.

Symbolism in Tribal Communities: In certain Namibian communities, knives have symbolic roles, used in traditional ceremonies or given as part of rites of passage. For example, a young man may receive a knife to signify his transition to adulthood and readiness to contribute to the community.

Hunting and Bushcraft: Namibia's wilderness makes knives essential for bushcraft, hunting, and self-sufficiency. Many Namibians use knives to prepare game, gather firewood, and navigate the rugged environment, relying on them as vital survival tools.

Artisan Craftsmanship: Namibian artisans create knives with wooden handles and simple yet durable blades, often crafting them for everyday use. Some knives are decorated with carvings or local materials, reflecting traditional craftsmanship and cultural pride.

Botswana

The Ikalaka Knife: The *ikalaka* is a traditional Botswana blade used by the Tswana people, especially in rural communities. It is a multi-purpose tool, ideal for farming, hunting, and food preparation. The ikalaka is usually a straightforward, sturdy knife crafted for everyday utility.

Cultural Importance and Ceremonial Use: In some Tswana communities, knives are used in traditional ceremonies and are symbols of social standing and maturity. They may be presented as gifts during weddings, initiation rites, or other important occasions, representing strength, self-reliance, and community respect.

Hunting and Survival Skills: In Botswana, where hunting is part of both cultural heritage and subsistence living, knives are critical for skinning, butchering, and preparing animals. Hunters carry knives as essential tools, and these blades are often crafted to withstand rugged outdoor conditions.

Handmade and Durable Designs: Botswanan knives are often handmade by local blacksmiths and craftsmen, designed for durability and heavy use. Handles are typically made from wood, and the blades are forged for strength, making them well-suited to the region's rural lifestyle.

Zimbabwe

The Hunga Knife: The *hunga* is a traditional Shona knife with a straight, single-edged blade, commonly used by the Shona people in Zimbabwe. It serves as both a tool and a symbol of cultural pride, often used in ceremonies and passed down through generations.

Ceremonial and Symbolic Value: In Shona culture, knives like the hunga are used in ceremonies, including initiation rites, marriages, and harvest festivals. These knives are valued not only for their utility but also for their spiritual and social significance, representing ancestral connection and heritage.

Agriculture and Hunting Use: In Zimbabwe's rural areas, knives are essential for farming, hunting, and preparing food. Farmers and herders use them for clearing vegetation, processing livestock, and other tasks essential to self-sufficient living.

Artisan Skills and Decorative Details: Zimbabwean artisans create knives with local materials, often decorating handles and scabbards with carved designs. Some knives are crafted with decorative embellishments that reflect Shona symbols, adding an aesthetic element to their practicality.

Mozambique

The Panga Machete: The *panga* machete is widely used in Mozambique, valued for its heavy, curved blade suited to clearing brush, farming, and harvesting crops. In Mozambique's rural areas, the panga is indispensable, as it's used daily for managing dense vegetation and farming tasks.

Cultural Significance in Rural Life: The panga is an important symbol in Mozambique's agricultural communities, representing self-reliance and resilience. It's a tool every household in rural Mozambique relies on, and it holds cultural value as part of traditional life.

Hunting and Fishing: In Mozambique, hunting and fishing are common in both coastal and inland areas. Knives are crucial for preparing fish, cleaning animals, and performing other survival tasks. Fishermen, in particular, rely on knives for preparing nets and processing catches.

Practical and Simple Craftsmanship: Mozambican knives, including the panga, are generally simple and practical in design, made to withstand heavy-duty work.

Handles are often made from wood or plastic, prioritizing durability and functionality over decorative embellishments.

Zambia

The Bush Knife: In Zambia, bush knives are vital for rural and agricultural communities. These knives are similar to machetes and are used for clearing land, harvesting crops, and processing food. Farmers and hunters rely on them daily, and they are considered essential for managing the bushland environment.

Knives in Cultural Ceremonies: In certain Zambian communities, knives have symbolic and ceremonial roles, particularly in initiation and harvest ceremonies. Knives may be presented to young men as symbols of maturity and responsibility within the community.

Hunting and Fishing Traditions: In Zambia, knives are important for hunting, fishing, and preparing game. Knives are used to prepare bushmeat and handle fishing nets, reflecting the local reliance on natural resources and traditional practices.

Handcrafted and Durable: Zambian knives are crafted by local artisans, designed for heavy outdoor use. The handles are typically made from local materials, and the blades are forged for durability, allowing them to withstand the challenging tasks of rural life.

Common Themes Across Southern African Knife Culture

Essential Tools for Rural and Agricultural Life: In Southern Africa, knives and machetes are indispensable tools for agriculture, hunting, fishing, and bushcraft. They are used daily for clearing vegetation, processing food, managing livestock, and building, reflecting the practical needs of life in rural areas.

Ceremonial and Symbolic Significance: Many knives in Southern African cultures hold symbolic value. They are used in traditional ceremonies, initiation rites, and community gatherings, representing strength, maturity, and connection to ancestors. For example, the Shona hunga knife and the Okapi knife carry meaning beyond their practical use.

Martial Heritage and Warrior Symbolism: Although the martial use of knives has declined over time, some Southern African knives, like the Okapi, have historical connections to self-defense and warrior identity. Knives are sometimes worn or carried during ceremonies to represent protection and honor, particularly in warrior communities.

Local Craftsmanship and Durable Design: Southern African knives are often handmade by local blacksmiths and artisans who craft blades designed for rugged use. These knives are built for durability, with sturdy handles and high-quality blades that reflect local craftsmanship and resourcefulness.

Cultural Heirlooms and Generational Value: In many Southern African communities, knives are passed down as family heirlooms, embodying family history and heritage. These knives carry cultural value, symbolizing the continuation of traditions and the respect for ancestors.

Influence on Global Knife Culture

Southern African knives, particularly the panga machete and Okapi knife, have influenced the design of survival and utility knives worldwide. The panga's robust design and effectiveness in clearing dense vegetation have inspired similar machetes and bushcraft knives popular among outdoor enthusiasts. Additionally, the craftsmanship of Southern African knife makers, who blend practicality with aesthetic details, has garnered respect among knife collectors and artisans worldwide.

Summary

Knife culture in Southern Africa embodies a blend of practicality, cultural identity, and craftsmanship. Knives are essential for daily life in rural communities and carry deep symbolic value in many tribal and cultural ceremonies. Southern African knives continue to represent the resilience, heritage, and artistry of the region's diverse communities, serving as both indispensable tools and cultural icons.

Oceana

Knife culture in Oceania is distinct and shaped by the region's island geography, indigenous traditions, and the practical needs of daily life in both coastal and forested areas. In countries such as Papua New Guinea, Fiji, the Solomon Islands, and the indigenous communities of Australia and New Zealand, knives and blades hold practical, symbolic, and ceremonial significance. They are used for a variety of tasks related to fishing, farming, hunting, and cultural practices, often embodying local craftsmanship and spiritual beliefs. Here's an exploration of knife culture across Oceania:

Papua New Guinea

The Bush Knife and Machete: In Papua New Guinea, bush knives and machetes are essential tools, widely used for clearing dense vegetation, farming, and building in the jungle. These knives are long and sturdy, with heavy blades suited to chopping through foliage and performing various outdoor tasks.

Stone and Bone Blades: Traditional Papua New Guinean blades were often crafted from stone or bone before the introduction of metal. These knives were used for hunting, food preparation, and ceremonial activities. Today, metal knives have largely replaced traditional materials, but stone knives are still occasionally crafted for cultural ceremonies.

Ceremonial and Symbolic Knives: Some knives in Papua New Guinea carry ceremonial value, used in tribal rituals, rites of passage, or as part of traditional dance costumes. These knives are often decorated with natural materials, such as shells, feathers, and hand-carved wood, symbolizing spiritual beliefs or clan identity.

Cultural Identity and Status: Knives in Papua New Guinea can symbolize social status and clan identity, especially when adorned with intricate patterns or colors. Decorative knives or blades may be passed down as heirlooms, and the possession of a finely crafted knife can reflect an individual's social standing within the tribe.

Fiji

The Totokia (War Club): Although technically not a knife, the *totokia*, a traditional Fijian war club with a pointed, pineapple-shaped head, reflects Fijian martial culture. It was historically used as a weapon and symbol of strength and bravery in warfare.

The Bowai and Machete: In modern Fiji, machetes and knives are essential tools for farming and food preparation. Farmers use these blades for clearing land, chopping coconuts, and other agricultural tasks. The *bowai*, a smaller utility knife, is used in fishing and other tasks requiring precision.

Ceremonial and Spiritual Importance: Fijians use decorated knives and machetes in traditional ceremonies, especially in tribal gatherings, weddings, and religious rituals. These knives often feature engraved handles and scabbards, symbolizing Fijian artistry and cultural pride.

Gift-Giving Tradition: In Fijian culture, gifting a beautifully crafted knife or machete is considered a sign of respect and honor. Blades with decorated handles are sometimes given as ceremonial gifts, often to commemorate significant life events or to strengthen bonds between communities.

Solomon Islands

Traditional Spears and Small Utility Knives: The Solomon Islands' indigenous communities traditionally used spears and small utility knives for fishing, hunting, and protection. Today, small knives and machetes are common tools, essential for activities like building, fishing, and food preparation.

Carving Knives: The Solomon Islands are known for their intricate wood carvings, and knives play a crucial role in this artistic tradition. Carving knives are essential tools for creating traditional items like canoes, masks, and decorative pieces, reflecting the skill and creativity of local artisans.

Ceremonial Knives and Symbols of Clan Identity: In certain tribes, ceremonial knives are crafted with shells, bone, or teeth and may be used in rituals or as part of traditional dress. These knives carry significant cultural weight, symbolizing the heritage and identity of the clan.

Practicality and Outdoor Utility: Like other Pacific Island cultures, Solomon Islanders rely on knives for practical, daily use. Blades like machetes and bush knives are used for clearing land, hunting, and fishing, and are often carried as versatile, all-purpose tools in rural communities.

Australia

Indigenous Stone Tools and Knives: Indigenous Australian cultures traditionally used stone tools and knives for hunting, food preparation, and ceremonial purposes. Stone blades were shaped by chipping rocks and were used to cut animal hides, prepare food, and carve wood. In some Aboriginal communities, these traditional methods are still practiced for cultural preservation.

Cultural Symbolism in Aboriginal Art: Stone knives and tools are often incorporated into Aboriginal art and symbolism, reflecting the connection to land and traditional survival skills. These knives hold cultural significance, especially as they are connected to Dreamtime stories, the Aboriginal understanding of the creation and connection to the land.

Modern Utility and Outdoor Knives: In rural and outback areas, Australians frequently use utility knives and machetes for tasks related to farming, survival, and outdoor activities. Knives are commonly used in bushcraft, hunting, and camping, reflecting Australia's robust outdoor culture.

Self-Reliance and Survival: In Australia's vast outback and bushland, knives are seen as essential survival tools. Many Australians who work on farms or live in remote areas rely on knives for everyday tasks, and there's a strong bushcraft and outdoor community that values high-quality survival knives and machetes.

New Zealand

The Taiaha and Mere: Although primarily short weapons rather than knives, the *taiaha* (a traditional Maori weapon with a pointed end and flat striking surface) and *mere* (a hand-held club) hold deep cultural significance for the Maori people of New Zealand. These weapons are used in ceremonial dances and represent honor, strength, and warrior spirit.

Everyday Knives for Farming and Fishing: In rural New Zealand, knives are essential tools for farming, fishing, and bushcraft. Many New Zealanders use knives and machetes for outdoor tasks, especially those who work in agriculture or engage in fishing and hunting.

Bone and Greenstone (Pounamu) Carving: Maori artisans create traditional carvings from bone and *pounamu* (greenstone or jade), often using knives to craft intricate patterns and symbols. These carvings, which may include small knives or dagger-like tools, are significant in Maori culture and are considered spiritual objects.

Cultural Heirlooms and Family Significance: In Maori culture, traditional weapons and knives are sometimes passed down through generations, symbolizing ancestry, family history, and cultural pride. These items often carry sacred meaning and are treated with respect as representations of family heritage.

Common Themes Across Oceania's Knife Culture

Essential Tools for Daily Life: In Oceania, knives and blades are practical tools necessary for daily survival. Knives are used for agriculture, fishing, hunting, and crafting, particularly in remote or rural areas where self-sufficiency is essential.

Martial and Warrior Tradition: Weapons like the taiaha, mere, and totokia are symbolic of Oceania's warrior culture, representing strength, honor, and identity. These blades and weapons are part of traditional combat training and ceremonial practices, reinforcing the values of bravery and resilience.

Ceremonial and Spiritual Importance: In many Oceanic cultures, knives and blades carry spiritual and symbolic weight. They are used in ceremonies, traditional dances, and rituals, often symbolizing protection, clan identity, or ancestral connection. Some knives are considered sacred and are passed down through generations as cultural heirlooms.

Artisan Craftsmanship and Cultural Art: Knives and blades in Oceania are often decorated with intricate carvings, engravings, and natural materials like shells and feathers. Artisans create knives that reflect local symbolism, and the blades often feature patterns and designs unique to each culture. The craftsmanship embodies the region's artistic heritage and deep connection to natural resources.

Gift-Giving and Social Status: In some Oceanic cultures, giving a knife or weapon as a gift is a sign of respect, friendship, or honor. A finely crafted blade can signify social status and cultural pride, and it's often given on special occasions or as a rite of passage.

Influence on Global Knife Culture

Oceania's knives, particularly the bush knife and machete, have gained recognition for their durability and practicality. These knives are used by outdoor enthusiasts and bushcraft practitioners around the world for their reliability in rugged terrain. The taiaha and kris have also influenced global martial arts communities, where practitioners study the techniques and cultural significance of these weapons. Additionally, Oceania's traditional knife-making methods and decorative styles have inspired artisans worldwide, particularly in the use of natural materials and indigenous patterns.

Summary

Knife culture in Oceania is defined by a mix of functionality, cultural symbolism, and artistic expression. Knives are essential for daily tasks and survival in island and coastal settings, but they also carry deep spiritual and cultural meaning. Whether as practical tools or ceremonial items, knives in Oceania represent heritage, craftsmanship, and resilience, reflecting the values and way of life of the region's diverse communities.

About the Author

Tom Sotis is the world's leading edged weapons instructor recognized as a special subject matter expert to international and US federal agencies for his specialized expertise in the use of weapons.

Internationally, Tom's work experience includes, but is not limited to: Cambodian Special Forces, Danish Law Enforcement, Hellenic (Greek) Coast Guard, Mexican Federal Police and Prison Guards, New Zealand Prison Guards, Norwegian Law Enforcement, South African Military, Police, and Security Forces, and Spanish Law Enforcement.

Domestically, Tom's work experience includes, but is not limited to: US Intelligence Agencies, US Special Forces, US Secret Service/ERT, Federal Bureau of Investigation, Drug Enforcement Administration, the Internal Revenue Service, and the New England Organized Crime / Drug Enforcement Task Force.

On the state level, Tom has trained numerous State Police, SWAT, Defensive Tactics Instructors, Municipal Police Departments, County Sheriffs, and Corrections Special Response Teams. While he continues to train Law Enforcement Agencies, Tom serves on the Palm Beach Sheriff's Volunteer Marine Unit.

Tom is a Personal Safety Consultant who has taught in 25 countries, the founder of Invincible: Performance Optimization Coaching, a Motivational Profiling Analyst, an engaging speaker, an avid traveler who has visited 40 countries, and an author of fiction and non-fiction books.

www.TomSotis.com

Other books by Tom

Unbreakable Honor

The Way of Tactics

Alexander the Great

History of Greek Warfare

Badass Warriors of Personal Combat

Understanding Our World

Global Crime Syndicates

Bounty Hunters

Nightclub Security

The Science of Motivation

Scientific Athletic Motivation

The Character Code

The Art of Character

Timeless Wisdom

Being a Good Man

Truly Safer